# Keeper'sBook™

FROM THE EDITORS OF KEEPERS AT HOME MAGAZINE

Keeper'sBook™

Volume 4

## Penny Wise

Helping You Be a Better Steward of the
Resources God Has Given You

He that is faithful in that which is least
*is faithful also in much:*
and he that is unjust in the least is unjust also in much.
Luke 16:10

Keeper'sBook™ series focuses on specific topics relevant to *Keepers at Home* readers. Our goal is to bring together talented writers who have passion for the subject and readers whose lives will be blessed by the information presented in each Keeper'sBook™.

Editor: Marvin Wengerd
Design: Valerie Miller

Keeper'sBook™ is not sold by subscription. To subscribe to *Keepers at Home* magazine call 1-800-852-4482 or write to: *Keepers at Home, 2673 TR 421, Sugarcreek, OH 44681.*

ISBN: 978-1-933753-43-0

2673 Township Road 421
Sugarcreek, OH 44681
1-800-852-4482
Fax: 330-852-3285

**Carlisle Press**
WALNUT CREEK

# Table of Contents

*Continued on next page*

# Table of Contents Cont.

# Penny Pinchers

## SHEILA J PETRE

I have a confession to make about plastic jugs. I can't pitch them out. One of my favorite "grocery extras" is one-hundred-percent juice. We all enjoy it. But then there is the problem of the jug. It's a fine, strong, two-quart jug and could be so useful for so many things. I can't bring myself to get rid of it. The *Organization Keeper'sBook*™ has a poem on the back about getting rid of leftovers. The author doesn't know if it's concern for world hunger, or ancestral thrift, but she "can't summon the nerve to dispose of these bits till their time has been served."

She's talking about leftovers. What about something which does not mold eventually? Which simply piles up on countertops, in cupboards, under tables, in small unused spaces in the garage, on top of freezers, in the attic…air enclosed in plastic, saved forever…some with lids, some without.

Which brings me to the lids: dozens of them, convening in the drawer by the silverware, getting in the way when I hunt for the pickle fork, popping out when I put away the measuring cups…

And I can't pitch them out. "I'll recycle them for you someday," my husband says, after battling sixteen empty jugs back into the pantry cupboard the morning he had gone on an innocent search for leftover chocolate. "I'll put them in the recyclable bin when I go to the dump this Saturday."

"You'll recycle them?" I cringe, knowing how useful they are, wishing I could recycle them myself, in any number of creative ways. But I bravely say, "That's fine with me!"

*I'll look the other way when he does it, I think. Maybe I'll be in the basement sorting aluminum foil pans.* ●

# Pinching
# PENNIES

MRS ALLAN MARTIN

In February 2013, the Canadian government stopped manufacturing a one-cent coin. Apparently the cost of producing a penny was 1.6 cents. While I don't need a calculator to figure out that penny making wasn't profitable, it is a little sad. How can we Canadians pinch our pennies if we don't have any?

Just what is penny pinching anyhow? The definition in my *Webster's Dictionary* is not too flattering—"stingy." And the meaning of the word stingy? "Refusing or being extremely unwilling to give any more than a very small amount." (Hmmm… perhaps it is good that we can't be penny-pinchers!)

Actually, pinching pennies is an expression we use to describe the careful use of money. The motive of this Keeper'sBook™ is not stinginess, but rather to encourage each other to be wise stewards in our homes. A steward is a manager, acting for the owner's best interests as far as he is able. Our money and possessions all belong to God. He allows us stewardship over what He has entrusted to us. What an awesome responsibility He gives! Thus the reason for pinching our pennies or trying to live frugally is because we don't want to carelessly squander God's material gifts.

You can pinch pennies without actually having a coin in your hand. A penny saved is a penny earned. When you go shopping (especially if you have children along), take a jug of water along so you won't need to buy something to drink. I prefer not to shop on an empty stomach, as I'm more likely to throw extra food in the shopping cart when I'm hungry. I like to follow a detailed, carefully planned shopping list for all the stops I plan to make while I'm in town. This saves time as well as money.

Another way I like to save money is by staying at home. Staying home not only saves on gas and vehicle expenses, but I'm much less likely to spend money at home. Not attending open houses or in-home parties also saves money.

Our motive for pinching pennies must never be for the sake of getting rich. The Bible tells us that the love of money is the root of all evil. A teenage friend was telling me about her indecision at the mall. "I really liked this coat, but it was so expensive! I could hardly decide if I want to part with that much money," she confided. "Then I remembered that money is the root of all evil anyway. I thought I might as well have the coat rather than the money." She had missed a part! It's not the money that is evil, but rather the love of it.

My mom has been a good example to me of wise stewardship. When I was growing up we lived frugally and tried to save or do without. However, when it came to giving, Mom was sure to be generous. As a young girl, I puzzled over this. Why scrimp and save only to give it away? Now I treasure her example. Let's be thrifty on ourselves but generous to others, "for God loveth a cheerful giver" (2 Cor. 9:7).

No, here in Canada we can't pinch actual pennies. But wait; perhaps we can pinch our nickels instead. Wouldn't that be more profitable anyhow?

*Every good gift* and every perfect gift is from above, *and cometh down from the Father of lights,* with whom is no variableness, *neither shadow of turning.*

JAMES 1:17

# Stewardship, Sense, and Self-Discipline

CONNIE BRUBACHER

"Charge them that are rich in this world, that they be not highminded, nor trust in uncertain riches, but in the living God, who giveth us richly all things to enjoy; That they do good, that they be rich in good works, ready to distribute, willing to communicate; Laying up in store for themselves a good foundation against the time to come, that they may lay hold on eternal life" (1 Timothy 6:17-19).

In the early years of our marriage, I had an experience which made a far-reaching impression on my spending and saving habits. We attended a household auction and bought a few boxes of assorted items. There were only a few items in each box which we really wanted. The remaining contents, to us, were garbage: flimsy Christmas tree ornaments, knickknacks, and odd glassware. As we were poking through our box lots, preparing to leave for home, the lady of the house walked up to us. Her white hair bobbed about her face in manicured waves and a matronly smile graced her face.

"If you don't want everything in those boxes take the rest to the thrift shop. They can sell it again. I hate so much to see things go to waste." Her eyes glistened with unshed tears as she spoke. "I was a child through the Depression. We ate bread without butter and porridge without cream or sugar. We were always hungry. Now it hurts me to see young people waste their goods. They don't know what it's like to be poor."

I nodded. My conscience smote my thoughts. Did I know what it was like to be poor? I would hardly say so. We were taught not to ask for needless extras, but we always had sufficient food and clothes. My heart warmed with grand intentions of not wasting one bit of the woman's goods.

As we sorted through the boxes at home I began to pile the unwanted things into one box for the thrift shop. My husband eyed the box decisively.

"We will not send that box of garbage to the thrift shop," he stated.

His firm manner brought my confusion to the surface. I was struggling with a false sense of guilt.

"If that lady was so poor in her youth, why did she ever spend her money on worthless things to begin with?" Indignation laced my words.

"That's the point. We are not responsible for storing her garbage just because she wasted her money on it." My husband's tone was final.

My conscience was still sensitive and shaky, but I took refuge in my husband's stability as I finished sorting the items and disposing of the garbage.

This lesson followed me through the years. I will not pretend that I have never made unwise choices when shopping, but the experience helped to mold my priorities.

### What Is Penny Pinching?

I used to carry a "pinches" opinion of thriftiness as hoarding every penny that comes along, wearing clothes down to tattered patches, and skimping on the bare necessities of life to save up dollars. There's a better word for this. I call it miserliness. The dictionary defines this as: "marked by grasping meanness and penuriousness." Penury, the noun form, is defined as: "a cramping and oppressive lack of resources or extreme frugality."

What does the word penny pinching denote to you? What are some synonyms of penny pinching? I chose frugal and stewardship, and checked them in the dictionary: "frugal: characterized by or reflecting economy in the use of resources; stewardship: the conducting, supervising, or managing of something, especially: the careful and responsible management of something entrusted to one's care (stewardship of our natural resources)."

Bearing in mind an attitude of sensible frugality and stewardship towards goods and gold, I will share a few more experiences and their practical applications.

### Bargains and Impulse Shopping:

We had stopped in at a discount store for a box of bulk cookies and crackers. As usual, there was much tempting ware on display. As I walked the aisles I spotted nice, soft tea towels. Yes, I had been thinking I should get a few more new ones, but it's the type of thing I seldom bother writing on my shopping list. I chose half a dozen and dropped them into my cart. Hmmm. The Band-Aids were half-price. In the last aisle were toys, games, and puzzles. Adorable pictures of capering kittens and bouncing puppies graced the puzzle boxes. I picked up a few, eyeing them dearly.

"Do we need those?" my husband asked at my side.

"No."

"So?"

I put them back.

As we placed our purchases onto the buggy, my husband muttered something about that "fifty-dollar box of cookies." I saw his point. We had stopped in to buy a bargain on bulk crackers and cookies. Impulse shopping can save dollars on the long run if monitored by good sense.

### Bulk Food and Fabrics:

Having mentioned bulk cookies and crackers leads me further into my "bulk" habits. I always buy staple groceries in bulk: 20 kg flour and white sugar, large bags of oatmeal and brown sugar, large-size boxes of baking powder and soda, salt and pepper, etc. I find if I keep the staples in stock I have less tendency to buy extras like Chipits and other rich dessert ingredients. The main reason is simply because I don't often need to go shopping.

Fabrics can also be bought in "bulk," if you sew your own coats and dresses. One of my area fabric stores has a deal that if you buy ten yards or more you receive a 10% discount. With three growing daughters and myself to sew for, I can easily use ten yards of dress fabric. The challenge is to discipline yourself to use those available discounts when the current new style of fabric is more pleasing to the eye.

### Minutes and Money at the Sewing Machine:

Most of us are taught the value of good workmanship, but there is another aspect of quality that is increasingly important in today's sewing world. We have a wide range of fabrics to choose from. There are flimsy cottons that will last only one or two summers, and there are durable, long-lasting polyester knits that will wear up to ten years. That is, if the thread holds them together. Cotton thread might last as long as a cotton fabric, but for the polyester knits and crepes, a stronger thread is needed. If you use cotton thread on a polyester fabric, you'll end up sewing the dress a second or even third time with your mending. Use a matching quality thread and save those minutes.

There are also the sewing machine needles to consider. There are microtex fine-point needles for flimsy polyester crepes. There are stretch-point needles for knits. There are solid jean needles for work fabrics. A jean needle will punch holes into a flimsy crepe fabric. Ask your local fabric salesperson to assist you.

### Food in the Fridge:

Our generation surely lives at ease. I sometimes recall a discussion with an older sister in the church. She was still well acquainted with the pre-electricity lifestyle when all fresh foods were carried to the cellar after each meal.

"It's so senseless," she stated forcefully. "The young generation has electricity, yet they let their leftovers spoil in the fridge."

I was amused at her way of saying it, yet I recognized it as a valid truth. A generation ago food sometimes spoiled because they had no means of properly chilling it. With our fridges and freezers we don't have that excuse. Many leftover meats and vegetables go together well as a baked casserole. Clearing the refrigerator of leftovers on a weekly basis is a good idea.

**Pretty Paints:**

When we moved onto this old homestead there was quite a variety of odd, partially empty paint cans in the cellar, yet none of the sensible colors were enough to do a room. When I wanted to paint a bedroom, I sorted the oil paints apart from the water paints and reviewed the colors. I soon realized the water paints had many shades of blue, red, and pink. *Hmmm...* My thoughts began to spin around the color wheel. If red and blue makes purple, would pink and light blue make mauve? I decided to mix it and find out for myself. The end result was a bedroom freshly painted with a pleasant rosy lavender. Note: Never mix oil-based paints and water-based paints. They do not mix.

We've covered a few aspects of saving dollars and cents. What about the other side of the coin?

**Disposables:**

What about the disposables? Paper towels, tissues, sanitary needs, wipes, and pampers. The efficient but expensive world of disposables tempts and taints our lifestyle. Are the disposables ever practical? If there is ever an aspect of penny pinching that demands self-discipline it is the field of disposables.

About a month before our fifth child was born I began to have serious bouts of false labor. It took very little exertion to stimulate the cramps. I could cope with simple kitchen duties like dishes and sweeping, but laundry day taxed my strength. At the same time our one-year-old was struck with a severe bout of diarrhea. Each bowel movement messed up her stockings, rubber pants, undershirt, and dress, and it happened several times a day. I was stressed and exhausted. It was mid-winter and I did not have enough housework to occupy a maid full-time. Would I just ask a maid to come on laundry days and risk spreading the flu bug to their household? Besides, I would still have the daily messes to clean up. I opted for the disposable route. It gave me several breaks. The snuggly fitting pampers prevented all-out leakage and I had two diaper-free laundry days.

Okay, you ask, did I make an extra trip to town for pampers? No, I had them in stock at home. That's the challenging secret to the benefits of disposables. Keep them in stock, but use them as little as possible.

**Tidbits of Free Advice:**

We drove into a horse tie-up shed one day at an implement dealer's. There at the side stood a wide, soft-cushioned, green leather armchair. Propped on it was a sign which read, "Free to a good home." We gave it a good home.

My husband and three-year-old daughter were driving home from a business errand when up ahead beside the road they spied a plastic play kitchen cupboard.

"Do we want that?" Dad asks Miss Three Years.

"Can we buy it?" she asked.

"We'll see. Maybe it's free. We will see if there is a sign."

There was a free sign standing on it. They happily brought the playset home. Now, a year later, our daughter still declares, "It was free, so we bought it."

In the early years of marriage my husband brought home a fridge magnet from a yard sale. (He picked it out of a free box.) Two teddy bears were pictured back-to-back surrounded by hearts. Beneath them was the statement: "Shopping makes life more bearable." I was embarrassed to display it, thinking it bears the attitudes of a spendthrift. Then came the winter I froze my toes while doing laundry. I couldn't rush to town and purchase a new laundry room, but I did buy new socks. They helped to make my life more bearable. The magnet motto took on a sensible meaning and I now display it unabashed.

So…are we misers? Or frugal homemakers? We can see that penny pinching like all other qualities must be balanced with temperance. Sensible penny pinching begins with a positive attitude of good stewardship.

MRS ALLAN MARTIN

# Insight from Grandma Martin

Thoughts about saving money and being a thrifty housewife invariably make me think of my maternal grandmother. Born in 1908, Grandma Martin lived through World War I and II and the Great Depression. Her folks were poor and could not always afford to feed and clothe their family. Thus, Grandma and her siblings took turns living with friends and relatives at times throughout their childhood. They helped their host family with the work in exchange for their board and meals. Now a mother myself, I realize how it must have tugged on Great-Grandma's heartstrings to let her children go. She scrimped and saved in ways we can't imagine today.

As a result of her childhood, Grandma had thrifty housekeeping down pat. I didn't always appreciate her advice as I could have, like the day she made me put the macaroni back on the stove to cook longer. I do not like pasta cooked to mush, but Grandma pointed out that the longer it cooks, the more it swells, thus feeding more people. Grandma knew how to stretch a meal. How good it tasted (or didn't) was beside the point.

Yes, Grandma Martin knew frugality. She passed away nearly ten years ago, but I still sometimes think of her words as I try to be a thrifty housewife. In Titus 2 the Apostle Paul told the aged women to be teachers of good things, and Grandma tried to do her part. Often she quoted sayings as a means of teaching us lessons about life. I'll share a few of her tidbits on thrift.

**Use it up, wear it out, make it do, or do without.**

In Grandma's day there were no Dollar Stores, nor disposable dishes and diapers. While these things are convenient (I use them too, sometimes), let's be careful what we throw away. I'm not suggesting you become a pack rat and hoard things that you'll never use, but sometimes we should consider a little longer before we toss. Let's look at each of these points individually.

**Use it up…** Is the milk turning sour? Make scalloped potatoes for supper or bake some muffins. If you don't have time today, freeze it in smaller containers to use in your baking another day—then make sure you don't forget! Are the carrots going bad in the cellar? Can or freeze them as soon as you can. While housecleaning the kitchen cupboards take note of food items that should be used up and incorporate them into your meals or baking soon. Scrape out the mayonnaise jar and squeeze the last bit of toothpaste from the tube. (At our house this is my job. The rest of the family goes on to a new tube and Mom sees to it that the old one is properly emptied.)

Last fall when I housecleaned I realized that a variety of cleaners had accumulated in my bathroom cupboard over the years. I decided not to buy any more cleaning products until I used up what I had.

When I rinse out dish soap and shampoo bottles with water to get the last bit of soap, I remember Grandma. Once she got a trial size package of dish soap in the mail, and made it last for four sinks of dishes. I chuckled inwardly as she scraped the inside of the package with a knife to get all traces of soap out. It was rather extreme, perhaps, but the principle was a good one—use it all up!

**Wear it out…** Many people prefer new clothes, but it's okay to wear old things too, provided they are not too thin and tattered. If you mend promptly and neatly, many clothes can serve you a long time. Grandma never got rid of clothes just because she or her children were tired of them.

Thrift stores are a good place to get clothing, especially for children. But remember to buy only what you need. The sweater that fits you perfectly is not a bargain if you do not need another sweater. My sister-in-law uses good, sturdy bedsheets from the thrift store to make everyday dresses for her daughters, at a fraction of the price of new fabric.

We have five boys, so pants are an item we need to buy frequently. I have learned that a good quality pair from the secondhand store will outlast new ones of a cheap brand. I save the backs of the pants that are worn out to be patches for others. Generally, I only patch them once. I don't like to patch patches. A few years ago I made two denim comforters for the boys' beds using the good parts of worn-out pants.

Eventually clothes do wear out. Don't be too quick to garbage them! First remove any hooks, buttons, elastic, or zippers that are still usable. Sheets and towels make good dishrags or cleaning cloths. Just cut them to the right size and hem. I cut old socks and other garments that don't make good rags into paper towel-size cloths and use them for one-time-use rags. They are very handy for wiping the grease out of the frying pan or to scoop up the egg Junior accidentally dropped. Just wipe and toss it in the garbage. Another use for clothes that don't make good cleaning rags is to cut them up for paint rags. Your friend who is renovating or building a new house might be glad for them. At home, we cut old clothes into strips and sewed them together to give to an acquaintance who wove rag rugs.

**Make it do...** Your son needs a new bike and someone offers you an older one that works fine. Junior had his eye on a new mountain bike. Can you teach him to make the older one do? You wish for a bigger slow cooker to make dressing for your guests. Could you bake it in the oven instead? The dresser that was left at our house when we moved here doesn't have nice drawer slides. The drawers tend to get stuck for the little boys. We'll make it do!

**Do without...** I cannot possibly understand this as well as Grandma Martin did. I have never owned only two dresses or had no footwear that fit my feet. I should ask myself more often as I shop, "Do I really need this?"

*A wife can throw it away faster by the spoonful than her husband can bring it in with the shovel.*

In our first year of marriage Grandma was at our place to visit for a few days. We chatted as I kneaded my bread dough. When I turned to wash my hands at the sink, Grandma gasped. "You're not going to wash all that dough down the drain, are you?"

I thought I had tried to scrape the dough off my hands, but I worked at it a little more. "Over time those bits of dough will make a loaf," she informed me. Then she quoted the saying above.

This saying came to mind again when I had a young friend helping me make salad. She cut thick slabs off the top and bottom of the tomato to remove the stem. A good portion of the lettuce head was considered waste. There was still a tablespoon of salad dressing in the spoon when she laid it in the sink. Grandma Martin would have been horrified.

My husband says the grocery bill is not what is going to make or break us financially, but to be careful in our kitchens is still good stewardship.

Keep after your fridge—don't let food spoil in there! I like to go through my fridge on a weekly basis and make sure we are eating everything that should be eaten. Plan ahead and incorporate leftovers from one meal into another meal. One mother I worked for said, "Don't call them leftovers, call them plan-overs."

Grandma taught me to peel and use the broccoli stem too. Just cube it and add to your salad or vegetable dish. The celery leaves and heart can be chopped and frozen to use in soups or casseroles if you don't want to eat them raw. While carrots and potatoes are new, just scrub them rather than peeling them. Not only do you have more of the vegetable, but the skin is also good for you! If the outer leaves of the lettuce are washed and refrigerated they will crisp up and be fine to use in the salad.

Buying staple grocery items in bulk can make a huge difference on the grocery bill, especially if you are feeding a large family. Avoid buying prepackaged food and make your own if you like the convenience of it. Make your own granola bars and cut them the size you want. Spread a long sheet of plastic wrap on the table and space the granola bars two or three wide evenly along it. Use a scissors to cut along the rows and soon each bar will be laying on a small square of plastic wrap. Wrap them up and put them in a box in the freezer for handy lunches. You can do the same with cookies and other dessert items. (Grandma would have packed things in reusable boxes, of course.) I like to make my own fruit-flavored yogurt or pudding and pour directly into lunch-size containers, enough for a week at a time.

*All the use you get out of something after it is worn out is profit.*

Did I hear you groan? It's not wrong to throw hubby's old work boots out (unless hubby isn't ready to part with them yet). Eventually things do need to be tossed. But the chair with the back missing may serve a useful purpose yet as a stepstool to climb onto the trampoline or to hold your laundry basket at the wash line. Since the handle broke off the wicker basket, you don't want to use it for baby toys anymore. Could it hold garden tools in the garage? The cracked container that no longer keeps cookies fresh in the freezer would make a fine sock box for Junior's drawer. And hubby's worn-out boot could be a chew toy for the dog or a pot on the back porch for your geranium!

Each week that you wash dishes with your old brush yet is not only "pure profit," but will enhance the pleasure when you finally purchase a new one.

On the other hand, there is no profit at all in having a garage or shed full of items that are worn out. It is a waste of time and space. Where the line is between holding onto potentially useful items and being a pack rat varies from one person to the next!

*Don't stretch out farther than your cover will reach.*

Grandma quoted this one in Pennsylvania Dutch. Directly translated it would be, "You must stretch yourself with the cover." In other words, live within your means. If we live on borrowed money, let's keep in mind that we must pay not only the cost of the items we purchase, but also the interest amount. Everything you don't buy will help get that mortgage or loan paid off sooner.

It's not how much you make, it's how much you save. In the world, mothers feel they need to contribute to the family income by having a career. This mentality of mothers trying to make money is also creeping into our plain circles. I don't mean women who assist their husbands on the farm or help run the family produce stand, though a woman may need to be careful there too. I'm talking about a separate business a woman runs by herself. When a wife and mother is trying to make an income, she ends up having to cut corners elsewhere. If she has less time to garden, can, and sew, will she still come out ahead financially?

(Not to mention what becomes of her husband and children's needs.)

"In my day, we didn't try to make money, we tried to save," my mother advised me as she noted women who try to help earn the income.

Help your husband make ends meet by saving, rather than trying to earn. It works much better with being a keeper at home, which is God's plan for us.

Moderation is the key in all things, including thriftiness. If you're in a busy stage of life and need to buy more convenience items in order to reach around, don't feel guilty. Back in Grandma's day they often had hired help for a year at a time, you know. However, I'm so grateful we can provide for our children's needs, rather than trying to figure out which of our relatives could afford to feed and clothe them for us. ●

# Substitutes for the Frugal
### LYDIA HESS

Instead of a funnel, create one from foil;

Cheap vinegar loosens some obstinate soil,

In place of a costlier Lysol. We swipe

A spill with a rag, not a use-and-toss wipe.

Black pepper with flour will substitute spray

To hustle some plant-loving insects away.

Dried beans work for stuffing, salt acts as a balm

For bee stings; petroleum jelly will be calm

Chapped hands, no elaborate lotion for now.

Need plant food? Try coffee. To banish wild fowl

From fruit trees, a snake-like hose mocks a decoy.

But, these have no substitutes: Love, Peace, and Joy.

# How to Save
# $124.34 a Day!

DIANNA OVERHOLT

*With input from over two dozen KAH readers*

I am a spoiled North American homemaker. I have an automatic washing machine, a dryer, an electric stove, a refrigerator, freezers, a vacuum sweeper, carpet shampooer, heavy-duty mixer, dishwasher (it came with the house!), and a four-slice electric toaster. I've even had an in-sink garbage disposal.

I am a blessed North American homemaker. According to the Bureau of Labor Statistics for our state, I am pocketing an average of $124.34 a day. This is not because of time- and energy-saving gadgets, but because of a far greater resource that God chose to give to me.

My children! (I think you guessed I would say that.) When King David calls children a "reward" in Psalm 127:3, "reward" literally translates as salary, compensation, wages.

Have you ever checked what you'd expect to pay someone to do the work that your children can do? Here's the average hourly wages for our state:

- Cook: $8.78
- Dishwasher: $8.67
- Maid/Housecleaner: $9.05
- Groundskeeper: $11.35
- Childcare worker: $8.94
- Gardener/greenhouse worker: $9.06
- Farm/Animal worker: $10.41
- Baker: $10.03

- Launderer/Laundress: $9.21
- Tailor/Dressmaker: $11.91

I was curious how much I was gaining by training my children to be competent adults. Figuring that it takes an hour to perform most daily tasks, I doubled the cooking, childcare, and laundry hours to arrive at a total of $124.34 per day that I'd need to pay if I hired workers.

"It is amazing how much work can really get done by children," Thelma Doerkson wrote, and I agree. It is our privilege, as mothers, to create an environment in which work is not seen as drudgery, but as an important part of family life in which each child has a place of service that only he can fill. Coryna Bucher reflected, "At our home, we try to take the chore out of chores! We stress that chore time should be referred to as 'service' to the family. After all, Jesus came to serve and we should do the same."

"Children are happier if allowed to feel useful and big," Katie Mast said. If you think that you have untapped potential in your children, as I know I do, then start listing on paper every little job you can think of. Things like: wiping doorknobs, light switches, chairs, and toys; gathering hangers and taking them to the laundry room; vacuuming the sofa; sweeping around the woodstove; wiping shoes; sweeping down cobwebs; even taking everything out of a cupboard or drawer so that you can clean and organize it. Then designate a child to be responsible for each job, perhaps using one of the following methods:

### 1. Slips of Paper

This common method of writing down tasks on slips of paper for the children to draw remains a favorite among mothers!

"My children (five blessings, the oldest is seven) love to each have his own colored container with age-appropriate jobs written on slips of paper. It takes time to get these ready, but even the two- and three-year-olds enjoy this. I often add a special slip to each container such as, "Mama will read a story," or "We'll go on a bear hunt," or "Let's have a snack." Also, having their own bucket and rag does wonders to inspire them. We've decided that extra puddles on the floor are worth the values and time spent with the children." –Thelma Doerkson

"When our children were young they had lots of fun picking jobs on slips of paper out of a bowl. (If their ages varied too much, I'd divide appropriate jobs by age into colored bowls.) There are so many things that can be done in short order when the excitement is high and the race is on. Yes, you do need to oversee! The just-emptied wastebasket might land on its side under the desk—they can set it properly. And toss in a few fun papers: 'Count to ten backward,' 'Say your memory work to me,' 'Take a ten-minute break' (for older ones), and even 'Take a drink.' (We had one who loved to take drinks.) – Alverna Martin

One reader uses the drawing method to decide which room to clean first. "There are always rooms that badly need cleaning but are easy to pass over," she wrote. "So I write each room on a slip of paper, draw one, and we clean that room—no moving until it's done."

### 2. Lists

Lists are great for turning normally chaotic times into structured ones in which each one knows his part.

Alta Zimmerman suggests dividing weekly cleaning jobs among individual lists. Copy the lists and rotate them with the children each week.

"My boys like to have their very own job list—sometimes they staple it to a piece of cardboard sized to fit in their pockets. I find it helps to break down the cleaning into small jobs so that each job doesn't take long and their enthusiasm doesn't wear out," writes Mrs. Jeremiah Martin. "I also use a list on the refrigerator to jot down after-school jobs that I think of throughout the day. The children check the list, and sometimes have fun doing the jobs before I ask!"

"Mornings before school, I find it works best to have a written list for each of the children working with me in the house," Sharon Burkholder writes. "It frees me to work with the children, chatting with them instead of constantly giving directions to someone."

Here is a good idea from Vera Hursh: "When my children could read, I printed up a paper detailing in simple language every little thing I expected them to do in each room. It was numbered in the order they should do them. With their names and a few pictures illustrating their tasks, it was special to them. We put the list in a plastic sleeve and kept it with our cleaning supplies. They took it with them as they cleaned. At one time there was a separate paper inside the bathroom cupboard using the ABCs to clean the bathroom. 'A' said, 'Gather the supplies' (which were listed), one letter said, 'Clean the mirror and give yourself a smile,' and 'Z' ended with, 'Put the cleaning supplies back in their place.'"

Several readers mentioned the type of cleaning list that my children also like to use. List every waiting task on a piece of paper, and let each child sign his name by the one he wishes to do. When the task is finished, he crosses it out and picks another one.

### 3. Cleaning Card Game –Rosanna Zimmerman

"It's Saturday forenoon. That means it's cleaning game day! My boys, ages seven, six, and four, eagerly assemble around the kitchen table while I sort the game cards. Each game card (made of a recipe card) has a picture drawn on the blank side with a caption explaining what the picture represents. On the reverse side, I numbered each card with 1, 2, or 3, meaning the order of importance in which the cards are to be drawn. The cards are placed facedown, and each player then picks a card (choosing 1s first) and does the job.

"Do I help? In the beginning, I used to pick a card too, but I've learned it works better just to manage and tie up the loose ends. I usually sort through the cards before we start, and take out the ones that don't need to be done that day, or the ones that I prefer to do myself, like 'Bake something' or 'Water flowers.' However, since the bake card is the most coveted card, I sometimes let them pick it! They just have to wait until I have time to help them later in the day. That also ends the squabble of who gets to help Mom bake!"

### 4. Pocket Chart -Cheryl Horst

"Tired of telling your children every work assignment? Try this solution that I learned from Brandy Clayton.

1. Cut and sew a double piece of material for the chart. Mine is 15" tall and 28" wide, but size will vary according to the number of children.

2. Write the children's names along the top. I used fabric paint.

3. Cut enough 4" squares of material for two per name. Sew two rows of these pockets across the large piece of fabric, with two pockets under each name. It is ready to tack onto a wall!

4. Cut pieces of paper for the pockets, 1" to 2" taller than the pockets, and narrower. Write down a job or draw a picture of it on each slip of paper.

"At work time, Mom fills the top row with papers and announces, 'Chore-card time!' Each child puts his papers in the pocket below when finished."

Coryna Bucher made a simpler variation of the pocket chart by using envelopes. "I wrote our chores on the back of regular envelopes (one chore per envelope) and taped the front of each envelope to the wall. Then I made cards with each child's name, making sure that the names would stick above the tops of the envelopes. These name cards are inserted into different envelopes every day, and each child is responsible for what his envelope tells him to do."

### 5. Poster Board Charts

There are many variations of charts with grids or graphs for putting stickers or check marks on completed tasks. These seem to be very effective, especially with young children. I bought a poster board that was marked with days of the week from a teacher supply store. It is our current method, and it is working well. Susie Mast makes two charts each year: one before school starts, and one at the end of school for their summer schedule. She uses a different color of ink for each child's tasks, eliminating the need to write their names. That way you only have to look at one spot of the chart to see what each child's task is for the moment, as opposed to having an individual box for each child and looking at several boxes to see what each is to be doing. We also like her method of having the same dishwasher the entire day, the same table setter, etc. It doesn't always work for every child to do every task, and that's where I fill in.

### 6. Magnetic Marker Board

Jackie Ladomato uses a magnetic dry-erase marker board system for daily planning that would work well to create a chart for children. Jackie says, "My husband came up with a system that has freed my mind and enabled me to be more productive. We bought a large magnetic white marker board (35" by 37") and hung it in the kitchen. Using dry-erase markers, and a yardstick to make straight lines, I divided my board into three categories:

- Today (for the tasks that need my attention today)
- Regular Tasks (for those things, such as mopping, that need to be done fairly often)
- Running To-Do List (for those things that don't necessarily need to be done today, and are not really regular tasks, but that I would like to get to sometime—organizing the front closet, scrapbooking a page, etc.)

To list my tasks, I made tabs by cutting index cards into eighths. I used a permanent marker to list one task per tab, and attached a magnet to it. I can easily move a tab to any column and put it in any order of priority that I need to! And because it is a marker board, I can also jot down with dry-erase markers tasks that come to mind, such as calling a certain person."

A marker board would be a sturdier, more permanent solution than a poster board, and one could easily draw columns or squares for children on it, with tasks written on magnetic tabs. Extra tasks could be written in (and then easily erased) each day.

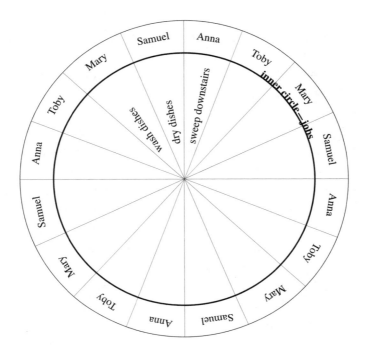

### 7. *Cleaning Wheel –Miriam Yoder*

"These wheel charts (above) work well for our family of nine children. We use two wheel charts: one for daily tasks and one for our weekly cleaning. Each wheel is made up of two circles, one a little smaller than the other, and held together in the center with a brad.

"On the outside edge of the bigger circle, I write a child's name in each section. The smaller circle has the jobs written in each section. These wheels can be adjusted with more or fewer sections, depending how many children you have and how many jobs. If you have four children doing jobs, and the wheel is divided into twelve sections, each child's name will be on the chart three times, which means they will each have three designated jobs.

"Our daily wheel gets turned every day. Our weekly wheel is bigger, divided into eighteen sections, and is turned once a week. The jobs don't need to wait until Saturday, they can be done any time of the week."

"Do I have to work?"

"No, not if you want to," I tell my children when they complain.

Twila Wenger writes, "If you like your job, you don't have to work... it will be fun instead! As a child I recall fun times helping Mom with the housework. When Mom had folded laundry stacks ready to be put away, my brothers and I with outstretched arms, representing a skid loader with forks, would scoop up the stacks and deliver them to designated locations. We often included sound effects and thought the work was grand! The same method worked for bringing laundry in from the line and clearing the table after meals. As I currently find myself blessed as a wife and mother, I enjoy incorporating fun work for my little people."

If you want more ways to nurture enjoyment and keep enthusiasm up, or ideas for a change of pace, keep reading.

"When my girls were learning to dust, I hid pennies around the room in places that were to be dusted. 'If you dust properly, you will find ten pennies in all,' I'd tell them." –Ruth Weber

"To spice up the weekly cleaning, make a treasure hunt for the children. Tape a job on each item to be cleaned, and on that item, say, a chair, is their next job. When they are all done, they get a slip of paper telling them where the treasure is." –Alta Zimmerman

"For a change of routine from using slips of paper, have them pick up and put away a certain number of items. I'll announce, 'For every ten items you put away, you get a gummy bear, or a penny, etc.' They work fast and look for things to put away, even on the counters and furniture." –Becky Schwartz

"'Every one pick up ten things!' I'd often say at clean-up time to my children when they were young. The number of items by the number of children really makes the work go fast! It still takes supervision, though. I caught one child picking up and putting down the same object." –Mimi Stoltzfus

"When my children were younger, they enjoyed playing Five-Minute Pickup. I would set the timer for five minutes and we would all pick up as fast as we could for five minutes. It was a short enough time to hold everyone's interest, yet long enough to make a difference. Sometimes we used five minutes while waiting for my husband to come in for supper, or five minutes before time to leave for somewhere." –Teresa Flora

"A cleaning game we enjoy: Fix a bucket of warm, soapy water and give each child a rag. Then name the child and the object to be washed." –Faith Zimmerman

Edward, my oldest, invented our cleaning tag game that the children revert to when clean-up seems to drag. Anyone can tag anyone else who doesn't have anything in his hand. So the object is to stay focused on picking up and putting away. If they place a glove in the coat room drawer, they quickly look for a toy or something on the floor to take with them. The house gets cleaned fairly fast!

### Working Ideas

"On cleaning days I give the children one or two laundry baskets and send them through the house to pick up everything—toys, books, dishes, stray socks, etc. It's amazing how quickly the whole place looks better. When that's done I can sweep and mop in a short time. Later they sort everything and put it in the proper place." –Laura Miller

"My mother divided the main area of the house into sections, according to the number of children old enough to help. We were then responsible for a room (or rooms) an entire week. Every morning we would go through our rooms, pick up toys, clean surfaces, and sweep. The person responsible for the bathroom made sure all dirty clothes were in the hamper, and washed the sink, countertops, and cupboard. Suddenly cleaning was not so distasteful. After all, it didn't take long to straighten up only one or two rooms! (We of course had our other daily jobs, too, such as fixing our beds and washing dishes.)" –Sharon Beachy

"My children have assigned rooms for the week, with a daily check-up time before Daddy gets home. If someone else causes a mess in your room, you can politely ask that person to clean it up, although you are responsible to see that it happens. They all know that while Daddy won't say anything if things are messy, he will quietly start picking up toys and that means they didn't do a good enough job!" –Lois Graber

"I give my children cleaning solution in a spray bottle instead of a bucket. That way no water gets dumped by energetic people or

crawling babies! If their rag gets dirty, they just get a clean one."
–Dorcas Bear

"Saturday mornings we often don't eat breakfast until 9:00 or 10:00. If the children are up by 7:30, most of the cleaning is done by breakfast time and everybody has a good feeling."–Barb Hege

"A home-school speaker suggested that instead of having your children rotate jobs every week or so, keep them on the same job long-term and it becomes much faster and more automatic for them." –Teresa Flora

### Well Done!

There is a simple way to reward children, and it costs nothing: Praise them! "Praise is a reward that can hardly be overdone," Ruth Weber observes. "Children love to please."

"Reward children for diligent effort," Sharon Burkholder stated. And not, may I add, as a bribe. I like the small rewards already mentioned. Here are more that can be interspersed throughout a work day:

- Treat everyone to a glass of lemonade
- Call Grandma to say hello
- Read one chapter of a book
- Play with the baby for five minutes
- Stand on the porch and sing a song
- Pass out Popsicles to everyone

Obviously, involving our children in household chores is about so much more than being thrifty or saving money. It's a way of life in which children learn things such as belonging, serving, teamwork, diligence, and responsibility—things that enable them to faithfully serve in God's kingdom.

It's still fun to imagine that I'm saving $124.34 a day! Yes, I'm spoiled. But mostly, I'm blessed. My children are a reward-gift from God and no price can be attached to that.

# Mismatched
# Butter Plates

EVA MARTIN

**M**anaging my own money when I came of age was my delight. While some people enjoy handling their own money so they can spend it freely for whatever they like, I was the opposite. I got pleasure out of seeing how little spending I could get away with.

I just loved walking down the store aisle to see what was on sale. Should I buy sugar while it's on sale or will it be on sale again before we need it? Would it be better to pay more for dark cocoa powder or take the cheaper light cocoa powder of which you need more? And what about margarine? Should I get the cheap kind? I read the label. Reduced calories. No, that was not good. Reduced calories are okay in some things, but not in margarine. The cheap kind, I concluded, has too much water in it. I can stir my own water into the margarine if I want to stretch it.

I did the arithmetic and figured out the price per cup of basic baking ingredients. That way it was easy to tell exactly how much cheaper a batch of cookies was when I used white sugar instead of brown sugar and chicken fat instead of vegetable oil. After all, I liked to know where every penny went. I soon decided chocolate cakes were too expensive to eat regularly. Applesauce cakes were much cheaper. So we ate applesauce cake, not because we were so poor, but I got a pleasure out of keeping the costs down.

Sometimes I baked cakes on cookie sheets to cut down on baking time. I pressed cookie dough into pans and cut it in squares to make the most out of the heat in the oven. All those spaces between drop cookies seemed a waste when cookie dough could just as well be baking in those spaces.

Of all my hobbies, penny pinching became my favorite one. Until... I discovered I had a bad habit. I liked penny pinching too much.

Part of what made that secondhand shopping spree so memorable was that it was on my birthday. The sun was barely over the horizon when we started out that Saturday morning. The van purred along and I leaned back in my seat enjoying my coffee and my friends. I was wished a happy birthday half a dozen times that morning and I had no doubt that wish would be fulfilled. How could my birthday be anything but happy when I was going secondhand shopping?

The secondhand stores were not open yet at that time of the morning, but we hoped to find lots of interesting garage sales first. Emma and I sat in the back seat chattering about one of our favorite topics—penny pinching. "Every penny I save goes toward new cupboards I'm looking forward to having someday," Emma confided. "Thinking of that motivates me to be thrifty. You know how the saying goes, 'Save where you can, then spend where you want to,'" she said with a laugh.

The day was full of happy surprises. I found several pieces of material large enough for dresses at the first garage sale we attended. At a secondhand store I found a pair of nearly new Sunday shoes. They fit me perfectly and cost only a fraction of their original price.

Towards noon, everyone had lost the eager step they had early that morning. We were warm and tired and ready to head home. "Let's stop in at one more store," Emma suggested. "They might have the treasure of the day. You never know what you missed if you don't check it out."

Emma and Joyce were still rearranging things the van when Louise and I entered the store. "Oh, look here!" Louise exclaimed. "A box of free stuff!" Emma just might find her treasure of the day here. We dug through the assortment of faded teddy bears, stained clothing, and chipped dishes. "Here's a pair of glass butter plates," Louise said. "Do you need them?"

I shrugged and shook my head. "I think I have enough," I said.

Louise nodded. "It's the sort of thing most people have enough of." We left them there and entered the store.

Just before we reached home Joyce plopped a package on my lap. "For your birthday," she said. "I know we generally don't give each other birthday gifts, but this was too good a chance to miss."

"Peanut butter!" I exclaimed. "The perfect gift. You know how much I like peanut butter."

Before I had time to say more, two more packages landed on the seat beside me. The package of garden geranium seeds had to be from Louise. She knew I admired the row of pink and white garden geraniums she had along the edge of her garden last summer.

"And this must be from Emma," I declared, as I carefully peeled back the tissue paper.

The pair of glass butter plates that emerged from the crumpled paper left me temporarily speechless. I was certain I had seen them before. "Thank you, Emma," I managed to say.

We let Emma off the van first. "Thanks a lot for the ride," Emma said to Joyce. "I guess you were planning to go shopping anyway, so you probably don't expect us to help pay for the ride."

For the second time I was speechless. I knew Joyce. She would never have gone to so many secondhand stores by herself. She was generous and took us wherever we wanted to go. We had put in a lot of miles, and considering the price of gas, it wasn't fair to expect her to give us a free ride.

When we got to Louise's house she quietly got out her wallet. "I want to help pay for the gas," she said. I admired Louise.

I wasn't feeling very talkative by the time I got home. I paid for my ride, piled my purchases on the sunporch, and plopped onto the nearest chair. Emma had given me a lot of tips on saving money that day, but just now, saving money didn't seem very important to me.

My mind was busy as I studied the two glass butter plates in my hand—Emma's "treasure of the day," I supposed. Here and there, the plates had a tiny chip on the edge. Although the two plates appeared identical at first glance, I noticed now that they didn't match and one was slightly larger than the other one. Obviously, Emma had given me the cheapest gift she could find. Maybe she would have felt guilty not to give me a birthday gift since the others all did.

Those butter plates are priceless. I have them among my most prized possessions, because they were precisely what I needed that day. Those mismatched butter plates made me think deeply and gave me a glimpse of what a selfish penny pincher I was.

Whenever I see those butter plates, I am reminded that I want to practice good stewardship, not so that I have money left to spend on myself, but so that I can help the less fortunate. ●

He that is faithful in

that which is least

is faithful also in much: and

*he that is unjust in the least is*

UNJUST ALSO IN MUCH.

If therefore ye have not

*been faithful in the*

UNRIGHTEOUS MAMMON,

who will commit to your

trust the true riches?

Luke 16:10-11

# UNDERSTANDING
# Sales Cycles

SUE HOOLEY

When navigating the grocery store, one is sure to notice all the colored tags proclaiming sale prices or items attractively displayed on the end caps. Exactly what is a good deal? How do you know when something is at its lowest price? Understanding sales cycles will help stretch your dollar in the grocery store.

A sales cycle in grocery shopping indicates when a particular product goes on sale. This means that it is likely at or near its lowest price. Virtually everything at the grocery store has a sales cycle, which determines the price of a product. Buying a product at the top of its sales cycle can cost you as much as 100 percent more than when buying it at the bottom of the cycle. For example, a 100-ounce jug of All laundry detergent sells for $9.99 at the top of the price cycle. At the bottom of the cycle it is only $4.99.

Most everyday products have an average sales cycle of about eight to twelve weeks. A 42-oz. box of Raisin Bran Crunch usually costs around $4.29. A sale price of $2.00-$2.50 is likely the lowest amount and a similar deal may not be available for several weeks/months. Paper products, cake mixes, baby items, and dairy items are just a few of the many products that have an eight-to-twelve-week cycle.

Some items, like barbecue sauce, hit their lowest price only once or twice a year. It seems odd that prices drop during seasonal demands, but it is part of a marketing scheme to get you into the store. For barbecue sauce, that is usually in the summer months when people are grilling. Stocking up on barbecue sauce for $1.00 a bottle will save you money when it costs $3.49 in December.

If you are used to buying groceries as you need them, the concept of buying ahead might seem complicated. Shopping the sales cycles is comparable to buying fruit in season. Most fruits are available throughout the year, but usually the price is better when we buy them in season. Just as we buy sensibly when produce is less expensive in the summer, we will buy sale items prudently. Be careful to honor store policies and be courteous to fellow shoppers.

We use around six gallons of milk per week. At $2.60 a gallon, that amounts to $15.60 a week or around $200.00 quarterly. Buying items on sale generates enough savings to cover that expense. Using the current Safeway sale flyer as an example, here are a few items that are on sale.

> Folgers coffee, $6.88, a savings of $4.00
> 1 gallon ice cream, $4.00, a savings of $1.00
> Peanut butter, $1.99, a savings of $.80
> 1# macaroni, $.75, a savings of $.25

Buying a three-month supply of the mentioned items would be a savings of $16.00 on coffee, $6.00 on ice cream, $4.80 on peanut butter, and $1.50 on macaroni. For our family, that is a total savings of $28.30 on only four items for one quarter.

I used to purchase all of our toiletries at Wal-Mart because I assumed they offered the lowest price. In some localities, that might be the case, but our local grocery store offers the same items at sale prices. For example, Arm and Hammer deodorant is consistently $2.29 at Wal-Mart and $2.79 at Safeway. Often Safeway runs a sale for $1.49, but about twice a year they have a three-week sale when it is only $.99! Considering the number of users in our household, that is a significant savings in a year's time! To my surprise, the same savings can be found on toothpaste, shampoo, and bath soap.

If this is a new concept, don't spend $500 immediately. Instead, designate a small amount of money each shopping trip to buy extra of those heavily discounted items which you will use sometime in the next few months. Neither feel obligated to get every deal. There will always be another sale on paper towels, mushroom soup, or potato chips.

Most sales are directly related to holidays and events. Sales, or the lack of sales, are also geared toward our mental framework. Cereal is generally more expensive in December—think about it; folks are probably going to buy cereal regardless of the price because they are in a hurry. However, Chex offers some of the best prices in December because folks are making party mix. If you use much cold cereal, consider stocking up in September, since back-to-school sales include cereal. Dieting is often a New Year's resolution, and in January there are many low-price options.

I've limited my choice of grocery stores to those that are closest to areas we regularly frequent. My only local possibility is Safeway. In the city thirty-five miles from home, I mainly shop at Fred Myer (similar to Kroger), Cash and Carry (restaurant supply store that is open to the public), and Costco (similar to Sam's Choice). Cash and Carry and Costco offer biweekly/monthly sales as well as volume buying. In this area, Fred Myer has tight competition, and like Safeway, they offer power buying. On sale, an item might be $2.50, but if four items are purchased the price drops to $2.00 each.

It took time to figure out which stores in the city were best for our shopping needs. The options were overwhelming, so I finally took a day for price comparison to establish a base guideline. After observing the sale flyers and visiting the stores repeatedly, it was easier to identify the low-price point.

Depending on your stage of life, this way of shopping may not work for you. (Our six children are ages 5-21.) Many of the young mothers in our area are Winco and Wal-Mart loyalists. I well remember the days of loading and unloading small children, and a shopping trip was less stressful if everything could be purchased at Wal-Mart. But neither did we consume as much food, and one tube of toothpaste lasted a long time.

Some type of budget will give you the ability to track your spending and saving and set parameters so that money doesn't slip through your fingers. A set amount of money designated for household/grocery needs will give freedom to creatively operate within those boundaries.

To find a workable budget, average your grocery spending from the last six to eight weeks and use that figure as an initial grocery budget. Over time and with practice, you will reduce your original grocery budget amount and you will stretch your dollars for a growing family. Remember: it takes time. You won't cut your grocery bill significantly in one month. However, if you find savings of 10% here and 20% there, within nine months or a year you will notice a difference. As a rule, buy only what your budget and storage space allow. You do not want to spend your total weekly budget on mayonnaise, ketchup, and sugar, and not have enough left to buy milk and eggs.

Sometimes storage can be a problem. Before I had a place for extra boxes of cereal, they resided in a bedroom closet. We added a few cabinets in the laundry room, but still not all the extras are at one location; rather they are here and there. The key is keeping supplies somewhat organized so taking inventory is stress-free.

The grocery store is where money goes fast for many households; we have to eat, so slight price increases are usually overlooked. However, there are incredible savings available to you when you buy products on sale. Understanding sales cycles will make stretching your dollar a pleasant sort of challenge.

*Here is a basic list of yearly grocery store sales cycles:*

*January:* snacks, chips, salsa, soft drinks, diet foods, medicines, soup

*February:* chocolate, breakfast foods, National Canned Foods Month

*March:* Frozen Food Month, household cleaners *(time to start spring cleaning)*

*April:* ham, baking items, eggs *(Easter)*

*May:* condiments, meat, cheese *(grilling season begins)*, tortillas, beans

*June:* *National Dairy Month,* grilling condiments, drink mixes

*July:* party items *(July 4th)*, ice cream

*August:* snacks, juices, school supplies

*September:* back-to-school sales continue, breakfast foods

*October:* candy, baking items start to be on sale

*November:* turkey, stuffing, baking supplies, *Black Friday sales,* soup, Jell-O, tissues, medicine

*December:* ham and turkey, baking supplies, chocolate chips, party items

# A Penny Saved

ANONYMOUS

"A penny saved is a penny earned." Who among us has not been brought up by these words? Sometimes, I think, in the affluent times of easy wages, this thought is so easy to push to the back of our mind. And yet, it is not our money, but the Lord's. If He has blessed us, it is in turn our duty to bless the lives of others. (Even if we feel we do not have any to spare, remember the widow's mite.)

Many a hardworking man is financially unstable because of his wife's spending habits. On the other hand, many young men have been blessed by a thrifty, hardworking wife. Into which category do I wish to belong? I'm sure we all want to be a blessing to our husbands and families.

Some women make the mistake of thinking they need to try to do all they can to add to the income. Really, this is in the man's place, and we can do just as much by watching for ways to save.

Needs and wants are two different things. I may want to have baby wipes, paper towels, and tissues at my fingertips, but do I need them? No, not if I consistently cut old rags and scraps into small pieces. These make great disposable wipes for all occasions—changing baby, wiping runny noses, spills, etc.

I want cake mixes, boxed cereals, and other handy items stocked up on my pantry shelves. Do I need them? Let's see. Cakes made from scratch are more healthy and also more economical. I can make my own granola cereal, which the children can learn to enjoy too. Learn to make big batches at one time and store in airtight containers or glass jars.

Most foods such as crackers, breads, and cookies can be refreshed by toasting in a hot oven for a few minutes. Older bread can be cubed and toasted and then used for toppings for salads or casseroles. Older crackers can be crushed and added to meatloaf. Homemade cookies gone stale can be crumbled and used in place of graham cracker crumbs. Use your imagination and be very slow to throw food away.

A nutritious, economical drink for children is to use whatever fruit you have on hand, and blend with cold milk. The family cow is priceless. Make your own butter and yogurt.

Table scraps can be fed to your chickens if you have them. If not, throw the scraps in the kitchen garden. It's a valuable compost for your soil.

When sewing and you have small pieces of cloth left over, cut them into square blocks and toss into a bag. When you have enough blocks (all the same size) this is a great way to teach your girls how to sew. Simply piece them together and make a blanket or comforter, which they may want to use on their beds, or you can donate to a charity.

Don't go shopping when you're hungry. Make a list beforehand and try to stick to it. Better yet, try not to go shopping too often. Of course, all children do enjoy occasional snacks and treats, and there's nothing wrong with buying them every once in a while.

Children don't need lots and lots of toys to be content; in fact, it often works the opposite way. With fewer toys, they will use their imagination more.

Give them scissors and glue, a cut-up magazine and paper, and they'll be occupied for awhile. Accept their drawings and pictures with thanks and pleasure. They are learning to give!

Old greeting cards can be cut up to make new ones. Children enjoy helping with that.

Something else that can keep preschoolers occupied for hours is empty cardboard boxes—several lined up in a row to make a train. One big box can be the house. Windows and doors can be cut out to make it realistic. Their imagination knows no bounds!

Yes, the possibilities are endless on ways to buy less and save more. Let's beware, however, lest we fall into the other side of the ditch and become stingy. Let's not hoard our money, but rather use it wisely to help others as we see fit. We cannot take it with us when we reach that heavenly home. How blessed we shall be if we hear the merciful words, "Well done, thou faithful servant." ●

# Ledges for JOY

SHEILA J PETRE

Some people give ten percent, and no more. Some people give ten percent, and no less. Between these two groups of people is a vast platform on which Joy perches and sings. Unfortunately, she sings only for one of the groups of people.

Does giving have borders? Is it giving if it does?

Last week I watched, mesmerized, as a mother, Ruth, and a daughter, Barbara, weighed out two bunches of grapes. Ruth had seen grapes on sale. She bought some for herself and some for Barbara. When she reached home, she didn't know which were hers and which were Barbara's, so she weighed them. They weighed three pounds and ten ounces. She reached for her calculator. At ninety-nine cents a pound, Barbara's grapes had cost Ruth $3.59.

"It's three dollars and fifty-nine cents," Ruth told Barbara.

Barbara wrote it down carefully on a piece of scrap paper. She paid three dollars and two quarters and one nickel and four dull copper pennies for those two bunches of grapes.

Neatly, she cut off the ledge which Joy would have perched on.

Some think of Joy as a little bird. You may picture her any way you like. I picture her as a miniature five-year-old girl with a doll and a song, swinging her legs over the edge of the little chair or ledge she sits on, waving one arm, crooning occasionally, lifting a happy face to the God who formed her.

However you picture Joy, know this: she needs a place to sit. If Ruth had told Barbara, "Make it three dollars," and skipped the tedious weighing and calculating step, Joy could have perched on the fifty-nine cents and sung to Ruth for a full week without stopping. If Barbara had handed Ruth four dollar bills and said, "Keep the change," Joy could have perched on the forty-one cents and sung to Barbara for a full week without stopping.

Satisfaction is not this way. Satisfaction lives in sheltered places with borders, and is a worthy companion in his own right. Satisfaction comes from penny pinching—by patching old pants instead of purchasing new ones; by waiting for toilet paper to go on sale before stocking up. Satisfaction comes when we give ten percent, with a cheerful heart.

Theodore and Patrick were both taught to tithe. When Theodore brings home a four-hundred-six-dollar paycheck, he carefully chisels out forty dollars and sixty cents for the deacon fund. Later, when his brother stops by for a small loan, he scoops thirty dollars out of the deacon fund and tells him to keep it.

When Patrick brings home a four-hundred-dollar paycheck, he slices off fifty dollars for the cost of building a new school. Later, when his brother mentions needing a small part for his tractor, Patrick buys him one with part of the remaining three hundred fifty dollars; he spends two hours installing it, and he doesn't record either expenditure as a gift.

Both Theodore and Patrick are satisfied. They are both giving, and they are both blessed for their giving. But in Theodore's heart, "Satisfaction" sits lonely in his snug home. In Patrick's, "Satisfaction" shoves a window up, extends a hand through it to Joy, living on the ledge of ten dollars—or more!—outside. They sing together many anthems of praise.

The Bible says we are to give a full measure, pressed down and running over. Some give a full measure. Some give a full measure pressed down. Because each of these is still a measured giving, and the next step is in a category of its own, it takes humility and a certain ease of spirit to give a full measure, pressed down and running over.

In a way, also, it takes a change in habit. We are taught to save, to rinse out the tomato sauce jar, to only buy grapes on sale. We calculate our month's grocery expenses and tally the cost versus profit of a hutch of lop-eared rabbits. This is another matter entirely. This is frugality. Frugality, an art form, must end where giving begins.

If you have taught yourself, by necessity or otherwise, to be frugal, you may find that measureless giving goes against the grain. Change your grain here. You do not wash the baby with the same scouring brush you use to scrub the sink. Giving, as it also relates to flesh, to people, cannot be done either with the same lip-biting calculation with which spending is done.

God understands this paradox. "He that oppresseth the poor to increase his riches, and he that giveth to the rich, shall surely come to want (Proverbs 22:16). The rich in this verse includes all who supply luxury items which you can live without. Pay these—and come to want. The poor here is every individual, especially those in the household of faith, to whom we relate financially with a temptation to measure and be frugal—the young widow in the church, the employee on the work crew, the brother who borrowed money. If we oppress them, measuring the gift, depressing the wage, raising the interest, we will, contrary to our frugal gut feelings, surely come to want.

God not only understands the paradox, He commands it and will bless it. Be frugal: "Seest thou a man diligent in his business? he shall stand before kings" (Proverbs 22:29). Be giving: "Every man is a friend to him that giveth gifts" (Proverbs 19:6). There should be no frugality, no penny pinching, no penny counting, in giving gifts. When we give, we give pressed down and running over. We don't measure what runs over. We set a minimum—a measure, pressed down—but no maximum, measureless running over.

Somehow the grains which run over the edge are larger, sweeter, and more palatable to Joy than the ones squeezed into the cup. They are also more mobile. They dance on to the next person, full of song.

I saw a writing book at my friend Kathryn's house. "Is it interesting?" I asked.

"Yes. You may have it. Pass it on."

It was a breeze of blessing. I enjoyed it. I passed it on, saying, "Pass it on." If Kathryn had kept the book, its audience would have been cramped to one. If she had loaned it, she and I only could have read it, and perhaps additional friends of hers, in carefully selected numbers. If I had bought the book from her, its audience would have been cramped to two—Kathryn and me. Since she gave it, not measuring, running over, as far as I know the book is still traveling.

This is the beauty of giving. When I lay a gift in the hand of another, her hand must be open to receive it. Since it is open, she will release what is in it more easily.

Soon, it may become a habit to open the fist. Once Ruth and Barbara open their fists, they will learn how sweet it feels. Eventually, when Ruth purchases grapes for Barbara, she will say, "Forget it," and not even charge the three dollars. The next week, Barbara will give her sister-in-law a loaf of bread.

Finally their ledges on which Joy sits will grow so broad, she will no longer need to sit on the edge, swinging her feet. She will stand in the middle; she will call in her cousins and they will compose a choir. They will sing praises forever to the God who gave His love, His Son, and all heaven itself to those who could give without measuring their entire lives and still not repay Him.

Lay not up for yourselves treasures upon earth,

WHERE MOTH AND RUST DOTH CORRUPT,

and where thieves break through and steal:

But lay up for yourselves treasures in heaven,

where neither moth nor rust doth corrupt,

AND WHERE THIEVES DO NOT BREAK THROUGH NOR STEAL.

*Matthew 6:19-20*

# How Pennies Pinch

HETTIE MARTIN

What does it mean to pinch pennies? Why would I want to? I would rather buy chocolates, and eat them all myself. Too often when I try and pinch pennies, it's me that feels the pinch. Besides, aren't pennies obsolete?

One rule I try to remember: No pinching at others' expense.

*Food:*

In a land that has the world's highest obesity rates, am I contributing to those statistics? That pie may be good, but will it really taste better if I eat a second slice, when I don't need it? The triple scoop waffle cone at Dairy Queen may be tempting, but I could buy a large box of ice cream at the same price and share it. The money I spend on a single serving of french fries could buy a whole bag of potatoes.

Instead of buying that expensive cut of meat, we could get our protein from brown beans. They're basic, cheap, healthy, and tasty. I find that Cheerios, in spite of sounding cheery, don't taste better than their no-name counterpart. Then again, maybe we don't need store-bought cereal. Homemade granola is basic, cheap, healthy, tasty... ahhh like brown beans!

Then there are those "luxury" items. Mine are chocolate chips, nuts, cream soups, and instant pudding. (I should probably add coconut and raisins, but I do like to consider them needs.) You can make your own list. It's easier to do without the luxuries—if occasionally or always— they aren't in the house.

Sometimes it's hard to decide where to be frugal. Using the leftovers in the fridge sounds smart, but if you then have to buy expensive food to keep your dog from starving, it seems silly.

Last summer, with all the rain, we had a surplus of strawberries. We sold some at the bakery where we work. (They paid well.) One noon, after peeling apples all forenoon, I picked out a few peelings before they hit the garbage. I have a weakness for apple peelings, and since the apple dearth the other year, my craving has intensified. I was blissfully hoarding the juiciest, thickest peeling when my sister burst my bubble. "How miserly can you be? Here we have so many strawberries that we sell them, yet all the fruit you eat for lunch is their castoff apple peelings!"

Is this taking it too far?

*Clothing:*

I do think I know how to save on clothing, but...

I feel one should wear out footwear before buying a new pair, yet I own a long row of partly used shoes and boots, and I'm trying to justify purchasing that fantastic kind of boots.

I suggest one wouldn't need so many dresses, then discover that my closet is just as full as my sister's.

I read of a poor man who had only two shirts. When offered a third one, he refused it, saying it would only become moldy. One to wear while the other got washed was all he needed.

I don't know a thing about saving.

Except...

I wear those ten-dollar "hot paws" gloves to drive my horse. Whenever I buy a new pair, I put patches on the first two fingers. It makes the gloves last twice as long.

*Household:*

If Mr. Clean is twice as expensive as store-brand cleaner, it should be twice as effective. Is it? Or do I buy it for the same reason men buy John Deere—for the name and prestige? (My apologies to you that are clueless about John Deere, and to those who own John Deere equipment because it is better.) With some products, such as a vise grip, you may get a superior enough quality to warrant buying the popular brand, but that isn't as common as we might wish.

Does the prettier bar soap give you that many dollars more pleasure?

If so, why then, go ahead and buy it.

I find it entertaining to read the extravagant advertising on dish detergent bottles, about the lavender scent making dishwashing such a tranquil experience, and so on. Sometimes I even believe it. Usually, though, I prefer homemade soap for washing dishes. It isn't as hard on my hands (in spite of their ads), and because I can make it myself, it's cheaper. And I can save on hand lotion.

Just because the shopping list says Kleenex, doesn't mean I can't buy the facial tissue that's on sale. Using hankies would be even better.

I love to browse through bookstore ads, then not go to the bookstore. I tend to go to the public library or a friend's house instead. If I find myself borrowing a book several times, or still wanting a book a year or two after reading it, I may decide it's worth buying.

*Energy:*

In today's world one can find enough information on conserving that I hardly need to say anything. Still…

At our house we have a favorite saying: "Close the fridge door to think. It's getting cold here!"

Winter clothes have a purpose. Wear them. Turn down the heat.

Around here, firewood is plentiful. We sell it, so we may as well use it. In winter our little woodstove serves as furnace, cookstove, and water heater, all in one. I like to consider that efficient.

Turn off the lights when you leave the room. Actually, turn them off when you're in the room. Our kitchen is a tad less bright during the day without the lights, but we can still see. Yes, we do have the energy-efficient fluorescent bulbs, but we're talking pennies, aren't we?

*Landscape:*

If you have lavish flowerbeds just for the Joneses to look at, why not eliminate them? Use ground cover or low-maintenance perennials. Whatever. You don't have to spend hundreds on annuals every year. One can bring begonias indoors to overwinter. I have regal geraniums in hanging baskets which I bring indoors in the fall. They don't always survive, but it's worth a try. And the alyssum in with them are bushier next year.

*Travel:*

A great place to save is to totally skip the Bahamas Cruise. (You never were intending to go, were you?) Quality time with the children, which was what you wanted, can be had beside the creek in the sugar bush on your own farm.

Do I have to see the Rocky Mountains this year? Will I then also want to see the Alps? And Mount Everest? And Mount Kilimanjaro? And the Amazon River? And the Angel Falls? And the Nile River? And the Sahara Desert? And Paris and Rome and the Holy Lands?

*Time:*

They say time is money, so saving time should pinch my pennies.

If it's just to impress my friends that I make four icing roses on each mini cupcake for a potluck, I may as well forget it. They will only be eaten anyway. Or worse yet, not eaten.

When doing laundry, I like to put the dresses on hangers to dry instead of pinning them on the line. Then they are all ready for the closet.

Using public transportation? Have a notebook and pencil handy, and jot down notes or story ideas while waiting for the bus. Or write while you are on the bus.

Do I want to start reading that long novel now? My ten-minute break might turn into a half-hour holiday. Is the book good enough to spend my precious time reading it at all?

*There are more things I wonder sometimes. Four things I think I know:*

Pinch only yourself, not others.

Enjoy yourself while you're at it.

Don't let money rule you, whether you're saving or spending.

Write an article or story. It may not pinch pennies, but it might bring new ones to pinch.

Let your conversation be
without covetousness; and *be content with
such things as ye have:* for he hath said,
**I will never leave thee,
nor forsake thee.**
Hebrews 13:5

# Merely an Apple Pie

ANONYMOUS

Nervously, Jon cleared his throat. He ran his hand through his wavy brown hair, making him look more than ever as though he wore an unruly mop on his head.

Once more he coughed. "Dad... Mom... I'm thinking of asking a girl."

I glanced at my husband. He didn't look as surprised as I felt. I should have known. Just the way Jon had remained sitting on the couch after the others had gone to bed... He wasn't really doing anything, just fiddling with the cushion. Obviously, he'd been working up his courage. Yes, I should have known.

Before either my husband or I could think of anything to say, Jon forged ahead. "It's Betty. Betty Lehman."

That's when the real shock set in. Never, when I dreamed about our sons getting married, had one of Norm Lehmans' girls entered the picture. I just thought our boys would naturally find girls who were accustomed to a simple, frugal lifestyle that matched our own. My breath caught in my throat as I waited for David to say something.

"I see," my husband said, and in those two words I detected that his feelings were similar to mine. "Well, Jon, I'm sure you've prayed about this."

Jon nodded emphatically. "Lots, and nothing seems to be in the way. She's a nice girl."

"Of course," David said quickly—too quickly, I thought. Would he go ahead and give his blessing, just like that?

"Listen, Jon," he said. "This is all pretty sudden for Mom and me. Could you give us a chance to talk it over before we take the subject any further?"

Jon looked hurt. "Well, I guess, though I don't see why. I mean, she's a nice girl, so what's there to talk about?"

"Sorry." David managed a crooked smile. "Hope you can have patience with us as we fumble our way through this new experience, Jon."

"Sure." He got up and left the room abruptly.

I drew a trembling breath and stared at David. In the privacy of our bedroom I let out my feelings. "How can Jon ever provide the kind of life Betty's used to? Why, she's accustomed to having so much more than we are in the line of conveniences and furnishings... Where does Jon think he'll find the money?"

A chuckle escaped David. "Frances, you have to realize that a young man doesn't necessarily take financial realities into consideration once his feelings become attached to a certain girl."

"Okay, so he doesn't have to think of that now, but if they marry, he'll have to!" I persisted.

"I know," he said. "I understand your concerns. Thinking back to the early days of our marriage, I remember how much it meant to me even then that you didn't expect a life of luxury."

I was silent. I wasn't fishing for compliments. All I knew was that David and I both came from homes where life's amenities were not top priority, and our home together reflected that. "Can't Jon see the glaring difference in Betty's upbringing?" I questioned.

"Well, maybe it's not as glaring as we think," David offered slowly.

My shoulders slumped. I wanted to see things the way he did.

Still I quavered, "So I can't judge from what I see in the Lehman home?"

"To some extent, we can," he agreed. "Still, Jon's right when he calls Betty a nice girl. We are after all one in the faith."

"I know," I said humbly. "Maybe I'm too quick to judge."

"We'll pray about it," David decided. So we did, and came to the conclusion that we should not stand in Jon's way. However, we felt it was our duty to give him at least a glimpse of the obstacles we perceived.

David managed to be very tactful when he approached Jon the next evening. I listened as he warmly encouraged our son to look to God in this great undertaking. "Betty is a sister in Christ and we won't stop you from asking her. If at any time you realize her upbringing is too different from yours, well—courtship isn't cast on stone."

Talk about stone, Jon's face looked a bit stony just then. He obviously didn't appreciate the last part of his dad's advice. Tight-lipped, he said defensively, " I still think you're being judgmental. Why, you hardly know her."

"We want to learn to know her better," I said, and Jon gave me a relieved smile. Underneath his defensiveness he was still a boy craving his parents' approval.

Jon and Betty started dating. Right away, we learned to enjoy her visits in our home. She had such a pleasant personality! We were happy, along with our son, as we watched their attachment growing. Though we were never able to forget the reservations about Betty's upbringing, after two years we gladly welcomed her into our family as a daughter-in-law.

Through considerable pinching on our part, we were able to help Jon and Betty buy a small home. As far as we knew, Betty never complained about the tight quarters, even though the appliances and furnishings she brought from home looked incongruous in such modest surroundings.

Time passed. Occasionally I found myself biting my tongue to keep from saying something when I visited in Jon and Betty's home and noticed extravagances. I tried not to let them bother me. I tried to remind myself that Betty was only doing as she had been taught, and probably never dreamed how I felt about her liberal spending.

But my patient husband did get to hear about these things. One day I said to him, "Here we are, pinching every penny in order to help our children and give alms to the poor. I can't help but feeling hurt when I see Betty pouring money down the drain for useless and unnecessary things."

He nodded soothingly in agreement. As months passed and he kept hearing similar outbursts from me, David confronted me firmly one night. "Frances, we can't keep going on like this. Are we loving Jon and Betty as we should if we keep on complaining about them behind their backs? Something must be done."

His words brought me up short. I knew he was right. I knew my feelings towards Betty were careening off track. "But what?" I asked. "What should we do?"

"Well," David said slowly, "the Bible exhorts us to speak the truth in love. We probably should have a good talk with Jon and Betty."

I cringed at the thought. "I'm so afraid I would hurt Betty. She's such a sweet girl."

"Hmmm," mused David. "Well, if it's any relief to you, I guess I could just try talking to Jon."

"I would like that very much," I told him warmly. "And be sure that Jon understands that we truly love them."

David's smile was lopsided. "I feel as if I've been given a tall order."

He waited a few days for a good opportunity to be alone with Jon. That Saturday he went to help Jon repair some pasture fences. I prayed for David while he was gone, and could hardly wait till nightfall to hear how things went. "Did Jon accept the concerns you shared?" I asked the moment we were alone.

David swallowed. "Jon got me at a soft spot. He was near tears as he explained that Betty is having quite a struggle. Actually, both of them are. They long for a baby, but so far that privilege has been denied them."

A lump rose in my throat. I'd wondered how they were feeling about this.

"So anyway," David concluded, "Jon said he can't bear to deny Betty anything these days, or criticize her, because of her struggles."

I was silent. Something didn't seem right with that reasoning, but I hardly knew how to put it in words. "Earthly possessions aren't the key to happiness," I finally said.

David nodded. "Jon and Betty are taking a very immature view. I tried to point that out, but Jon started getting so defensive and his pain was so apparent, I couldn't bear it anymore. I just dropped the subject. Unfortunately, the rest of our afternoon together was a bit strained."

"Too bad," I commiserated.

We'd made an attempt, but had gotten nowhere. And the problem didn't go away. It haunted us like undigested food lodged in the stomach.

Betty and Jon's spending seemed to grow more uncontrolled. I nearly panicked when I learned how freely Betty used credit cards. How could they ever pay those bills, with the size paycheck Jon had? Things didn't figure anymore.

Then came the day when Jon asked to borrow money from us for an addition to their house. David told me about it in the evening. I cried out in dismay, "How can they think we have money for that?"

"It was a blow for me too," David confessed. "I hope I wasn't too blunt with Jon. I simply said we can't help them."

Our dismay only grew in the following weeks. Somehow, Jon was able to borrow money from the bank, and work was started on the new addition. Wanting to do our duty, when the foundation was put in we went to help with the concrete work.

But that day we realized something had changed. A rift had opened between our family and our son's. A coolness had developed, so real it was like an icy wind from the north.

Our hearts ached. Could this be happening to us? Between loving family members? Between fellow-believers in Christ? And all because of money?

We prayed. Again and again we poured out our hearts to God, hardly knowing what to ask for, feeling as though we groped in the dark. What was our duty? Even though we could not see our way through, we believed that our all-knowing, all-loving God surely had a way for us.

One day when the new addition was noisy with hammers and saws, Betty came over to me in the afternoon. "I've served the workers their coffee break, and I felt I need a bit of peace and quiet," she confessed, settling into a chair at the kitchen table.

"I'm glad you came," I said sincerely.

She requested a knife and a bowl, and joined me in cutting up apples. "Are these for pies?" she asked. When I nodded, she rushed on, saying, "I wish you would teach me how to bake an apple pie."

I stared at her. It had never occurred to me that she didn't know how. "Of course," I managed.

"You must think it is terrible that I don't know how," Betty said contritely as I showed her how to mix the crust.

"Listen, I don't want you to worry about how I feel," I told her honestly. "I'm just happy to show you."

Wistfully she said, "There are so many things I wish I knew. Thrifty things. Frugal things. Things I never learned at home."

I was dumbfounded. To think that here and now, while simply making an apple pie, a window had opened to send fresh air through the tensions between our families! With a heart swelling in gratitude to God, I said simply, "Betty, I'll be happy to teach you anything I can."

# Winning
## AT THE
## Grocery Game

CRYSTAL STEINHAUER

Rising food prices. A tough economy. We all feel our belts tightening to some degree. Grocery stores are no respecter of persons—whether shopping for a family of twelve or picking up food for one or two, sooner or later, we all end up there. Understanding a few marketing gimmicks may help you to stretch that grocery budget a little further.

Grocery stores may seem like an innocent jumble of food items, but every display is designed to get consumers to spend. Since everyone has to visit the grocery store occasionally, and many of us stop in frequently, grocers want to get every penny possible out of each visit, leaving you with a how-did-I-spend-this-much feeling, and them with a got-you-again grin.

The most essential tool for smart shopping is to know food prices. Is 2/$5 a good sale on butter? Should I stock up on chicken when it's $.99 a pound? Make a list of the items you buy often and pencil in the prices as you shop or copy the prices from your receipt. I make my list in a file in my computer, but a notebook would work just as well. Compare at several stores, if possible. You can see at a glance which store has the best price on a certain item and decide if a sale price is a steal or not.

Make your price record even handier by including a column to record the best sale price you've ever seen on an item. Make this price your goal—for example, I try not to pay more than $.78 a pound for chicken legs, $1.38 for chicken tenders, or $.98 for a pack of cream cheese. When I see my goal price, I stock up on the item. Prices vary from area to area, so your goal prices may be higher or lower than mine.

Which item is usually on your list, the thing you have to make an emergency run for most often? Unless you live on or near a dairy farm, it is probably milk. This most-purchased grocery item is usually placed at the back of the store so you pass by all the center bins and the end-of-the-aisle sales to reach the dairy section. How many times did you run into the store for one item and come out with ten? They got you again!

And speaking of end-of-aisle purchases, don't assume the items placed on aisle end caps are a good sale. Instead, walk down the aisle to where the item is normally sold to make sure you are getting the best deal. Is there another brand that's cheaper?

If you want to save big, look down while you shop. Vendors pay premium prices for the shelf space that's at eye level. Cheaper store brands are often on the lower shelves. (The exception to this rule is the cereal aisle. Sugary cereals are placed at a lower level to catch children's eyes.) Many times there's no difference in quality in the store brands versus the name brands—sometimes it's even the same product just packaged differently. The ingredient list can be helpful in determining the difference in products.

Another grocery store trick is to pipe smells from the bakery into the air. Studies have shown that pleasing aromas make you feel comfortable and at home, which increases the chance you'll shop longer and buy more. The enticing aromas also make you hungry and could convince you to make impulse purchases. BG's, a grocery store where I shop occasionally, has their bakery exhaust coming out at the front doors. They are known for the best doughnuts in the county, and it's pretty tempting to wander back to the bakery and check out the Boston cream doughnuts.

Details of a store's environment are planned carefully. Often they play slow, comfortable music to help you relax. Researchers discovered that the more slowly you move through a store, the more you buy. Even the type of floor can make a difference. Shoppers who went from a smooth floor onto a bumpy tile floor slowed down—and picked up more items they weren't planning to buy. Recently I stopped at Giant, a grocery store in our area that lives up to its name. I only needed a few items, so I grabbed a little cart and went zooming for the produce section. The floor was tile and what a clatter that little cart made! I slowed down and immediately felt my focus drifting to the display of Oreo cookies that said, "Only $1.88 with coupon!"

Above a display of Coke cases, a sign shouts, "Limit 4." Limits are placed on some items to make you think it's a super sale. People will often buy the limit even if they don't need that many.

Another marketing trick of manufacturers is to recommend that you use more of a product than you need. Picture the toothbrush on the Colgate boxes. How much toothpaste is on the brush? A good inch. A pea-sized amount would work just as well. Another example is the baking soda fridge packs. Arm & Hammer now recommends you change the baking soda in your fridge every month after years of saying to replace it every three months. What changed? Nothing, researchers discovered. Laundry detergent and dishwasher liquid are also examples of this. Two tablespoons of laundry detergent is enough unless your load is especially filthy and one teaspoon of dishwasher soap gets the dishes clean.

## Maximizing Your Grocery Money

If possible, look at the store's flyer before shopping. Often the front-page items are loss leaders—items the store is selling at a loss to entice you to come and shop. Make use of these items if it's something you need.

Shop at more than one store. Take advantage of the loss leaders and the lower-priced items at each store. If that means driving farther or buckling an extra round of car seats, this may not be a suitable option.

Find a discount grocery or dent-and-bent store in your area. I like to pick up canned goods and expired marinades and dressings at the dent-and-bent store. I've found most items are still good for a short while after their expiration date.

Dent-and-bent stores are handy, but it is crucial to know your prices when shopping there. When I first started shopping at discount grocery stores, I assumed everything was cheap and I stacked my cart full. When I did some price comparison, I was surprised to discover the discount grocery store doesn't have the lowest prices on everything. For example, sour cream from the discount store costs $1.29. From the local grocery store, I could get the store brand for $1.19, and they sometimes run a sale for 10/$10 ($1.00 apiece).

Make a list and stick to it. Impulse buying can be the number one destroyer of grocery budgets!

For me, impulse buying is much more of a temptation at a discount grocery store. I was telling one mother that I don't know if it saves me money to shop at discount grocery stores because so often I buy things I wasn't planning to. When I go to the regular store, I only buy what's on my list. She replied that those extra things she picks up at the discount grocery make special treats for her children's lunches or an added touch for supper. Know what you can afford.

Make a budget. Grocery shopping is one of the trickiest types of shopping because we are constantly making decisions that only differ by a few cents. Throwing a pack of bacon in the cart that costs $3.65 doesn't seem to be that big of a deal. A $.99 cappuccino from the snack bar to sip on as I drive home can't harm anything, but it is not hard to damage our grocery budget this way. If you have a hard time sticking to your budget, take the budgeted amount in cash, plus $20 more.

Take a calculator when you shop. It's an invaluable tool for figuring the unit price (check out the price labels on the shelves; many stores figure the unit price for you), keeping a running total, or comparing prices. One month, we had a few days left until the next paycheck and there was only $26 left in the grocery budget. I was determined I would not go over for once, so I entered every item in my calculator as I put it in the cart. I found benefits beyond helping me to stay within the budget. I had to look at my cart and decide which items were really important and which ones we could do without. The box of baking chocolate, even though it only cost $.99, went back on the shelf. Chocolate chips could wait until next week; I could make molasses cookies instead.

If you only need a few things, take a basket. You won't be as quick to buy a gallon of iced tea or a frozen turkey on sale if you have to carry it in a basket. Also, when your basket is full, it's time to get out of there!

Try to shop as efficiently as possible. Organize your list according to the layout of the store. This is a huge time-saver—you won't be trooping back to the produce section to pick up the forgotten onions. Shop when the store is empty—first thing in the morning is usually best—not over lunchtime or late afternoon, evenings, or Saturday. And never shop when you are hungry.

Be wary of coupons. Coupons are great money-saving tools, but they are usually for pricey convenience foods. If you have a coupon, make sure it's for something you would buy anyway and that the price is lower than its generic counterpart.

Do you often forget to bring your coupons when you shop? Salvage the envelopes from your junk mail and write your grocery lists on the back of them. As you clip coupons, slip them inside the envelope. Throw away expired coupons or ones for products you don't need.

Watch for good sales and make use of them, but remember to read the fine print. On Black Friday, I set out with my bargain-hunting nose to the ground. I stopped by a children's clothing store that advertised on a big red poster "75% off entire store." I was pleased to find some clothing I needed for my little girl and got in line to pay. When I finally reached the checkout, I discovered the dress was only 25% off. What had I missed? As I left the store, I studied the deceiving poster. What it really said was "up to 75% off entire store." I'd missed the fine print and was the loser for it.

Enjoy store samples guilt-free. There is one reason stores offer samples of their products: they pay off. If you take a sample and then feel obligated to buy the product since the sampler is there watching you expectantly, refuse the sample!

If there is a 10 for $10 sale, only buy as many as you need. Earlier I mentioned sour cream being on sale for 10 for $10. It would be foolish of me to buy ten cartons of sour cream just because that was the sale. I have a small family, and we would never be able to go through ten containers of sour cream before they spoiled. Rarely do you need to buy ten of something to get the sale price. (But if it's buy one, get one free, most stores do not give you 50% off if you just buy one.)

Buy bulk if you can, but watch the unit price; there are times when bulk is not a better deal.

If your grocery store has an ethnic food section, pick up your spices there. McCormick spices cost almost twice as much as a brand such as Badia in the ethnic section. The selection may be smaller, but they do have a lot of the common spices such as cinnamon or garlic powder. You may even find a new family favorite like fajita seasoning! Another cheap place to buy spices is a bulk food store.

Avoid prepared foods. Not only can you prepare it for less yourself, you can cut back on the salt, sugar, and additives.

Cut, shred, slice, and dice your own food. I checked the produce section at our local grocery store. The containers of watermelon chunks looked tempting—the perfect thing to add to a bowl of fruit. I glanced at the unit price—$4.78 a pound. Just for interest, I strolled over to the watermelon quarters. They were $.99 a pound—that's over four times less than the cost of the diced melon. Apples were similar—the sliced apples were $4.54 a pound, while a bag of whole apples was $1.59 a pound.

Don't buy things on display at the register. If you really need a pack of gum to take care of your coffee breath, walk back to the candy aisle and get it there. I noticed that a single pack of Orbit gum cost $1.19 at the register. A three-pack in the candy aisle cost $2.29, or $.76 a pack.

If you get home and are still beaten by the bill, try pulling out your receipt and circling the most costly items. Is there a lower-cost alternative you could try? Maybe steaks need to stay at the store and chicken take its place at supper time for a while. Or try making biscuit mix instead of buying Bisquick.

Go as long as you can between grocery trips. Impulse buying is not a problem when you're at home. Staying home also forces you to use up some of the food already in your refrigerator and pantry. And using up those items keeps you from throwing them away because they've spoiled.

One mother of seven shared that she shops on Monday. Since the store she frequents runs its sales from Monday to Monday, she can take advantage of both weeks' sales. Check your store's flyer to see which day of the week the sales change. Also, if the store ran out of an advertised item, ask for a rain check.

Cultivate a grateful heart. When you're tired of skimping, saving, and making do week after week, try cleaning out your fridge, freezer, and pantry all in one day. We have much—usually lots more than we realize!

With a little shopping savvy, you can learn to stretch those dollars a little further and come out the winner in the grocery game.

CHARGE THEM THAT ARE RICH IN THIS WORLD, that they be not highminded, nor trust in uncertain riches, but in *the living God, who giveth us richly all things to enjoy;* That they do good, that they be RICH IN GOOD WORKS, ready to distribute, willing to communicate; Laying up in store for themselves *a good foundation against the time to come,* that they may lay hold on ETERNAL LIFE.

*1 Timothy 6:17–19*

# A Frugal Lifestyle

MRS SILAS BOWMAN

Bef efore we are truly ready to practice frugal living, we need a solid reason for doing so. If our aim is merely for material gain—to become rich or to lay up treasures on earth—our efforts will be stunted.

Frugal living glorifies God. Our Anabaptist forefathers stressed a simple lifestyle, warning against sumptuous living in all areas, including food, clothing, home furnishings, and leisure time. This is an example we want to follow. Being conscientious in spending is good stewardship and should be our guide, whether we have much money or little. We should strive to pay our debts, and to lessen the burdens on others within the brotherhood and community. We want to have enough money to help the truly poor, in keeping with Ephesians 4:28. If we have children, not only do we want to provide them with their material necessities now, but also have funds available to start them off on their financial journey.

We have not been able to help our oldest sons start their farms. We are still struggling to get out of debt ourselves. Neither of our fathers were good financial managers, and it seems we have not learned it either. We have made some wrong decisions, we have suffered from restrictions placed on us, and we have not been as diligent as we should have been. But we have been blessed by a supportive, compassionate brotherhood, and have gained experience which may help others to live more frugally than we have.

This is no guide to financial management, but I would like to mention one point. Avoid borrowing money when at all possible. Interest gobbles up your money faster than pigs can eat their chop, and it brings no fatted pig to market. Invest where necessary, but do without, where you can, instead of borrowing.

Practice contentment. Concentrate on needs, not wants. Live plainly, without undue thought of what others in the community have. Do, however, follow their good examples and advice to frugal living.

Choose a healthy lifestyle. In some areas, this will be more expensive initially, but it will ultimately pay off. Avoid junk foods, processed foods, excessive sweets, and empty calories, whether they are cheap and readily available or not.

Strive to eat mainly what you grow. Don't fall for the philosophy that you need coconut oil from Central America or dong-quai from China. It can neither be economical nor as God intended for us to depend on food medicines grown half a world away. Use moderation and eat your own or your neighbor's grass-fed poultry, meat, and dairy products. Grow your own garden, or live off the seconds of the local produce growers that you trust. Learn to like your own garden-grown herbal teas and plain water instead of coffee and soft drinks. Teach your family by example and by word not to overeat.

If you have time and opportunity to do so, grow your own vegetables and fruits. Eat much raw or fresh in season. Learn to store and to preserve by canning, dehydrating, or freezing. Experiment with saving seeds. Collect your own flower seeds, and start new houseplants from slips. Be conservative with flower beds and houseplants. These can use much time and money if you aren't careful, and in excess may be more for pride than the beauty of nature.

If you raise produce to sell, be content with seconds and surplus as much as possible. Train yourself and your family to be patient, selling the first and best produce when prices are premium, then eating and preserving when supply exceeds demand. Be flexible. If one year the cucumbers do extra well, can more pickles. Perhaps another year you will have an excess of beans. When apples are abundant, use them creatively. When you have more strawberries than you can sell, eat more of them, and take opportunity to can or freeze an extra amount.

If possible, raise your own chickens for eggs and meat, and also other poultry. Consider the possibility of owning a good Jersey cow, which produces more for less feed than bigger breeds, yielding plenty of cream for butter. Learn to make yogurt and cheese. This can be as simple as cottage cheese or as challenging as cheddar. Make custard, milk puddings, and your own whipped cream. We have a German saying, "Eine Kuh deckt unser Armut zu." (A cow hides our poverty.)

Avoid processed and packaged foods. If you can find the time, bake your own nutritious bread and cookies. Make your own breakfast cereals. Consider the old-fashioned option of cooking oats, wheat, or corn for porridge. Do your own butchering, or purchase from your local slaughterhouse, by the quarter or whole carcass. Make you own luncheon meats—the variations are endless. If you need to pack many lunches, invest in good quality thermoses and serve hearty stews or simple creamed potatoes and meat.

Sew your own clothing as much as you can. This will vary according to time and talent. (I learned that it is more economical to pay others to sew our suits and coats. Others can do a much nicer job in half the time it takes me.) This can include underwear, slippers, mittens, coats, bibs, plastic pants, and diaper bags. Many in our community make their own children's stockings from bigger stockings or thin sweaters. Be on the lookout for inexpensive, good quality fabric, especially at reduced prices. Consider using good secondhand sheets, the darker ones for dresses or linings, the light flannel ones for diapers.

Keep after your mending, so you don't need to make or buy new articles of clothing sooner because too many are on the mending pile. Mend carefully, so the garment still is neat and serviceable. Be humble. Be willing to shop at thrift stores, to use secondhand footwear and mismatched furniture, and to stop at the share shed.

Reuse whatever you can. Instead of buying disposables, like tissues and paper towels, sew handkerchiefs and use worn-out towels and underwear for cleaning rags and throw-away grease wipes. Make dishcloths from tea towels. Be creative. Use worn or outgrown clothing for rag rugs. Cut scallops from wool coats, and blanket-stitch around them, using leftover yarn, matching or a mixture of colors. Sew these on a worn rug or heavy denim for a creative mat. Reuse snap lids and twist-on lids, cooking them ten minutes to soften the rubber.

Buying new fabric and cutting it to small pieces for patchwork quilts is not economical. Use the leftover new material from your sewing for the finely pieced parts. Use bigger pieces as plain blocks in between. Or consider sewing together large sections of plain inexpensive fabric with a matching or contrasting border. Quilting a pattern onto it will change it from a piece of cloth to a work of art. You can make pretty and serviceable winter-weight quilts with lightly used clothing. Cut up fleece wear for cozy blankets.

Consider sharing with a sister where you practically can. Discuss with a neighbors your plans to buy books and magazine subscriptions, and trade off with them. Be fair, though, and go the second mile in care and repairs. Offer some abundance of flower bulbs, herbs, or seedlings to your neighbor. She may have an extra supply of other varieties or colors. Unless you do huge amounts of canning, go in shares with another household for a high quality food strainer or noodle machine.

Learn to shop wisely. Go shopping less frequently. It gives you double the check on impulse buying, because you will have to buy more at a time, besides being tempted less frequently. Use a shopping list and stick to it unless you see one of your regular items on sale. Buy in bulk. Don't shop on an empty stomach…carry lunch. If you need to buy a meal, remember that the grocery store offers much more for less than a restaurant does. Buy good quality merchandise, rather than going for the cheapest. Don't run from store to store and from town to city to chase after the best bargains in small items. It isn't worth your time, your bus tickets, or your taxi fare. If you need to make a major household purchase, be sure to shop around some for the best buy. Remember that many stores carry their own in-store brands which are equivalent in quality but much less expensive than the cheaper brands. Learn to hunt them out; they are plainer and harder to spot, but are usually beside or between the pricey name brands. Learn what products are worth buying in the Dollar Stores and which ones are usually too cheap.

Be your own doctor where you safely and comfortably can. Read up on natural approaches (food and medicine), and experiment with home remedies and homemade salves and tinctures. Try burdock leaves, garlic, and apple cider for example. But don't postpone necessary doctor visits until they become an expensive emergency visit. (May God grant you wisdom to discern!)

Care well for what you have. Keep your tools and machines in good shape, clean and protected from damage. Put things away, not only to keep order but to avoid unnecessary wear. Practice making "a stitch in time" to prevent the need for major repairs. Weed your garden before it is hopeless. Pick and preserve your crops when they are ready, not after things are beginning to spoil.

Be thrifty and efficient with your time, and teach this to your children. Think ahead. If you need to carry empty jars to the cellar, consider what canned or stored goods you may need for your next meal, and bring them along. Have the girls carry and fold laundry upstairs when they go to make beds. As you put away the leftovers from one meal, plan how to incorporate them into one of the next meals. Before hanging one season's clothes away, tag them with suggested alterations for the next corresponding season. Jot down proposals for sewing and keep it in your sewing cabinet. Practice self-control. Don't spend hours dreaming over magazines and flyers that only promote dissatisfaction with your simple lifestyle. Be a good steward of your time as well as of your money. As long as you have time and energy, the possibilities for "making your own" are endless. Wasting too much precious time prompts you to take the easy way out and buy.

Don't feel guilty if time and conditions do not allow you to "make your own" as much as you would like. (We never have enough time, do we?) A healthy, relaxed mother is worth much more than a few saved pennies.

Keep your priorities straight. Your spiritual needs must come first, and that of your children. Consider their health and your own. Do not neglect your husband. Never compromise church standards to save money. Support your husband's work and wishes. Be careful that in your effort to live frugally you do not become a peevish, impatient mother or a critical wife. Invest in your children. Take time to love, to nourish and train them, and teach them life skills, including frugality and economy.

Read stories to them about poor families whose children were responsible for the housework while the mother was sewing or laundering for others, to help your children see that this is not unique to your family. But be sure you help with the dirty work too. You do not want to embitter your children by being unfair to them, nor do you want to set an ungodly precedent.

Practice thankfulness and a positive outlook. Remind yourself and your children of how much you have, rather than what you are missing. Read and think about the truly poor and suffering around the world.

These suggestions are only a small sampling of ways in which to save. Use the ideas as a springboard to find means that fit into your unique situation at this time. Do not be ashamed to ask others around you for suggestions and advice.

In all your efforts, do not make frugality a religion, keep it as a lifestyle. Neither let it be a constant weight on your mind. Try to relax, do your best, and accept your limitations. Some families are more blessed financially. Perhaps you are more blessed in other ways as you learn contentment and moderation in all circumstances.

*But ye have despised the poor.*
*Do not rich men oppress you,*
*and draw you before the judgment seats?*
*Do not they blaspheme that*
*worthy name by the which ye are called?*

James 2:6-7

# When Cardboard Won

## THE WAR

REGINA ROSENBERRY

It was spring. The air was alive with the excitement of warmer days and new life. This excitement swirled within me as I thought of working in my flower beds after the winter's hold. Gathering my hoe, I was ready to dive into the bliss of dirt when stopped by an ugly sight. My herb garden with raised beds and walkways was overrun with this horrible-refusing-to-die grass, the hard-to-pull kind of grass with strong runners under the soil. Hadn't I beat that evil grass with the hoe last year—chopping its roots and yanking its blades? But there it was, flourishing with every passing day. Must I resort to spraying chemicals on my own ground?

A few days later while waiting on my daughter at the orthodontist, I picked up a *Birds and Bloom* magazine. I read with interest an article about gardening with cardboard.

Hmmm, cheap cardboard. Something we burn or trash all the time. Layering my flower beds with cardboard to smother the weeds, something nontoxic—the idea appealed to me. I began to save every cereal box, cracker box, and even the butter boxes, and was amazed at how much cardboard I had thoughtlessly pitched every day.

After collecting a bagful of my ammunition I decided it was time to start: *Operation Down with the Grass*. First, I went against my organic preference and sprayed the grass with weed killer; this was an out-and-out war I was waging. A week later, my husband weed-whacked the grass off low to the ground. Now came the cardboard. Dragging out my trash bag full of boxes, I let the children have a grand romp tramping the boxes flat. I laid the flattened boxes in my walkways, covering the dead grass.

My husband came over to inspect my work and proclaimed it a hillbilly job. I said it was free and saving money. The only problem I encountered was finding out my bag of cardboard ammunition would not nearly cover my walkways. Where could I get more?

The next day while cruising the aisles at the grocery store, I passed a boy stocking the shelves with cereal. What did I see lying on his cart but lots and lots of large flattened packing boxes!

"Hey," I said. "Could I by any chance have that cardboard?"

"Sure may," he replied. "I'll take it up front for you."

I was as excited as if I had won a door prize. Back home, I carted my boxes out to my garden, ignoring my husband's rolling eyes, and continued my war.

My next step was hauling wheelbarrows of mulch and dumping it on top of my boxes. I spread the mulch evenly over the cardboard, hiding my free, hillbilly-like weed cover. I was delighted to let my husband know I didn't need to spread my mulch as thick as usual, hence saving his pennies. I surveyed my hard work. All that could be seen was dark mulch-covered walkways. Even my husband grinned and proclaimed it perfect.

My *Operation Down with the Grass* was finished. I hoped. Next spring, I'll see who won. In the meantime, I hope the worms are impressed that Mrs. Paul's fish fillets contain whole pieces of fish.

So while I was waiting to see how my cardboard would work, here are a few other cheap tips I experimented with.

• I layered newspapers in my flower beds before mulching them. It took longer to do my mulching, but in the long run it was well worth the extra effort, for I had very little weeding all summer, and my mulch stretched farther. In areas where I had problems with grass or thistles taking over, I used small pieces of cardboard (cereal boxes were a perfect size) for more protection with great results. Some organic gardeners would say the colored ink on printed cardboard (cereal boxes for example) may be toxic; other sources say it is not. To be on the safe side, I kept this type of cardboard for my flower beds and used plain shipping boxes in my garden.

• I placed large pieces of cardboard between my tomato plants and newspapers between the bean rows, then dumped grass clippings on top. The weeds must have been offended with receiving old news, for my rows were mostly weed free all summer. It all dissolved over the winter and couldn't be found when we plowed the garden this spring.

• Since I have a cousin who farms, I am delighted with access to old hay. It makes a wonderful mulch, and it also improves our poor shale soil. After cutting the strings, the hay bales separate into sections. I lay the sections down my garden rows and in my flower beds, and again very little weeding is needed the rest of the summer. Hay also keeps moisture in the ground and around my plants, and improves my soil by hosting many worm conventions (along with an uninvited six-foot blacksnake).

So now the winter has passed, and spring has come again. It is time I gather my hoe and go to the battleground. Ah-ha! No grass in sight. The free hillbilly cardboard wins. The worms seem happy. All is well. ●

# A Penny Wise
# Garden

*How to Have Your*
*Best Garden Yet, and Spend Less*

GINA MARTIN

**W**hat can be cheaper than gardening? With several dollars' worth of bean seeds, you can harvest buckets of green beans. A six-pack of tomato plants can provide fresh tomatoes for several months. One zucchini plant can furnish you—and your neighbor—with zucchini for a month.

But others have told me that gardening is not worth it. By the time they bought seeds, plants, tools, fertilizer, tiller, gas for the tiller, chemicals, and mulch—gardening was not cheap. And that accounting did not include their time.

My husband and I have compared what we spend on gardening to the large amount of fresh vegetables we harvest, and we consider it a worthwhile investment. The time spent working as a family in our garden, enjoying exercise and fresh air, while learning to grow our own food, is time well spent.

But sometimes finances are tight and every dime needs to be spent wisely. All of us would like to grow a better garden for less money. I will share a few penny-saving tips that I have gathered.

### Tip #1—Cultivate friendships with experienced gardeners.
If you are a new gardener, experienced gardening friends are invaluable. They can save you from making costly mistakes. Before beginning your first garden, have an experienced gardener look over your plot of land and give an opinion on how you should begin. If you

grew up with gardening, you may already have years of experience, but a more experienced gardener may still give you new insight.

I have an older friend who I call frequently with my gardening questions. Gardening books are helpful, but nothing beats talking to someone in your own area and climate with years of gardening experience. If I have a problem, chances are she has experienced it also, or at least has some idea of where to find a solution. As the old saying goes, "The cheapest experience you can get comes secondhand—if you'll buy it."

If you lack a real-life gardening friend, you'll have to learn from a gardening expert through books. I have a shelf full of gardening books, but the two I turn to most often are *Gardening When It Counts* by Steve Solomon and *The Vegetable Gardener's Bible* by Edward C. Smith. If finances are tight, check what gardening books your library has to offer.

Another good resource is your local extension office. You can find them under county government in your phone book. They can give you helpful advice, backed by research specific to your area. I have found them helpful in identifying diseases and blights that afflict my plants. It is reassuring to hear, "Your grapes have black spots, which we are seeing a lot in our area because of the humid weather conditions." (Maybe misery does love company.) Often the extension agent offers to mail me more information.

### Tip #2—Plan Wisely

A garden should begin with wise planning. In Luke 14, Jesus speaks of counting the cost before starting a building project, and gardens benefit from planning too. A common mistake of beginning gardeners is to make the garden too large. Evaluate how much time you can invest in making your garden a success. An overgrown garden in August will only demoralize your desire to try again the next year. Growing a huge market garden and letting it rot in the field is a waste of money and effort. Better to start small and increase slowly.

Evaluate what your family eats. Do you like to eat a lot of salad? Or do you want to freeze green beans? If no one will eat brussels sprouts or eggplant, don't bother to plant them. There is also a limit to how much a family can eat at one time. One family is unlikely to eat a dozen cabbages unless you plan to preserve them. Stagger plantings so your produce is not all maturing at the same time.

### Tip #3—Invest in Your Soil

Your garden plants will only be as good as the soil that sustains it. Time spent building up your soil will yield high dividends. Good soil produces healthy plants less susceptible to pests and disease.

Vegetables grown in nutrient-dense soil will also contain more nutrients.

If you are starting a garden in soil that was covered with lush vegetation, such as a lawn, or even a healthy crop of weeds, you can guess that the soil will contain the nutrients needed for vegetable growing. But if the plants growing on your future garden spot are thin and straggly, you will need to make amendments to have a good garden.

When it comes to increasing soil fertility, it is hard to give advice that fits all soils. (Another reason why a local gardening expert is helpful.) Almost all gardens can benefit from a light application of lime (50 lb. per 1,000 sq. ft.) in either fall or spring before planting, and lime is not an expensive soil amendment.

### Tip #4—Learn to Make Compost

One of the best amendments for all soil types is compost. Compost is perfect for the frugal gardener because it can be made for free with some work and time.

While whole books have been written on the topic of compost making, we make simple compost by piling up all our garden and kitchen wastes, such as vegetable peelings, grass clippings, leaves, and other plant material. We also throw in some chicken manure to add nitrogen and get the pile to heat up.

Typically we build a compost pile and just let it sit for months to let the microbes work, while we start another pile. To speed up the composting process, you can chop the plant matter up into small pieces and turn the pile frequently. The pile should stay slightly moist, but not soggy. With time, the plant matter will break down into brown, crumbly, dirt-like matter called compost. It can then be spread on the garden and worked into the soil.

### Tip #5—Buy Quality Tools, But Only What You Need

It can be tempting to walk through a garden supply store and think you need one of everything. It is better to find out what you truly need. A good garden can be grown with only a shovel, rake, and hoe, and maybe a file to keep them sharp. Choose high quality tools and take care of them; they will last for years. Check yard sales and secondhand stores for quality gardening tools for a good price.

A big tiller that can pulverize the dirt into soft planting rows may look fun and necessary, but count the cost of the purchase, upkeep, and repair of such a machine. It may be better to rent a tiller to break up your soil in the spring and use hand tools the rest of the year. Maybe you can barter with a friend who owns a tiller.

Seeds may not seem like a tool, but they are vital to the gardening effort. Never skimp on seed quality. Planting inferior seeds is not a way to save money. Typically, you can find far better quality and selection by mail order. Choose a mail order company from your climate zone. (Don't buy from a company in the South if you are in the North.) Look for a seed company that does their own seed trials and chooses to sell only the best seeds. Some suggestions—try Territorial if you are in the northwest US, Parks for southern US, and Stokes for the Northeast. Of course there are many other excellent seed companies.

### Tip #6—Avoid Chemicals

Even if organic gardening is not one of your goals, learn some organic techniques to avoid the high cost of chemicals. Do all you can to grow strong, healthy plants that will shrug off a few insects. Be content if you find a few imperfections in your vegetables and need to cut out a bug hole.

A minor insect problem can be controlled with hand picking. This has worked especially well for us with potato bugs. If we are vigilant in picking them off when they emerge in early summer before they lay their eggs, we can avoid a major infestation later in the season. Even if your skin crawls at the thought of touching a bug, stifle your shudders. We taught our young children the fun of picking bugs and dropping them in a bowl of soapy water, and now we have eager helpers.

Another simple technique to avoid insects and disease is to rotate your vegetables each year. Pests and disease can overwinter in the soil ready to attack next year's crop. If their preferred plants are not easily available, they may disappear. Some vegetables, like tomatoes and potatoes, are closely related and should not be planted after each other. A four-year rotation is ideal, but even a one-year break is better than nothing. If your garden area is divided into four areas, each year a different kind of vegetable can be planted. Group 1 could be potatoes, peppers, and tomatoes; Group 2 could include corn, squash, and cucumbers; Group 3 is the cabbage family; Group 4 is beans and peas. Onions, carrots, beets, and radishes may be planted among the groups. Of course, this is ideal, and difficult to do exactly. But even if your only goal is to not plant tomatoes at the same spot each year, you will benefit. Another advantage is that the nutritional needs of plants differ. Moving vegetables also helps to keep from depleting the soil of specific nutrients.

### Tip #7—Mulch

If "time is money" then a time-saver is also a money-saver. And mulch has saved us time—lots of time.

I was introduced to mulching when I married. My in-laws were avid mulchers. By the time I joined the family, they were semi-retired but still had a large garden. My father-in-law mulched with newspaper and grass clippings between the garden rows, and his garden was beautiful and weed-free with very little work. My husband and I soon adopted the practice of mulching for our own garden.

Watch for free mulch. Cardboard, newspapers, grass, and leaves are often discarded and readily available if you look for them. In the fall, my husband brought home truckloads of bagged leaves that were sitting along the curb free for the taking. After sitting over winter and partly decomposing, we used the leaves as mulch in the summer. If we would have thrown a scoop of manure in the bag in the fall, the leaves would have composted down even better. Soak newspaper in a tub of water first so the newspaper isn't blowing away as you spread it out. Avoid wood and bark mulch in your garden because it takes a long time to break down and will bind up the nitrogen as it decomposes.

It is best not to mulch too heavily in the fall if you plan to till in the spring. The mulch will not have time to break down over winter and will keep the soil damp and cold in early spring. Earth worms love mulch and will help increase your soil fertility. Mulch will also help keep soil moist and allow you to avoid irrigating over a short dry season. It is best to mulch after a rain. If you mulch dry soil, the rain may run off the mulch without soaking in.

### Tip #8—Make Your Own Liquid Fertilizer

Homemade liquid fertilizer, sometimes called manure tea, will give your plants a boost. And it is super simple to make.

Place your dry ingredient into a five-gallon bucket. I use chicken manure mixed with wood shavings, filling the bucket about a fifth full. Other manures will also work. You can also use fresh grass clippings, but then you should fill the bucket about ⅔ full.

Fill the bucket with water and let sit for three days. Stir about once a day. After three days, the nutrients should have seeped out into the water. Longer than that will just increase the stinky fermentation! Strain the liquid into another bucket. The strained "tea" needs to be diluted before using it to water plants. Dilute both manure tea or grass clipping tea one to one. Then pour it into your watering can and go find a hungry plant! Use it up in a day or two. You can pour any extras on your perennials or your compost pile.

Be careful you don't fertilize plants that are drought stressed. Water your plants first, then fertilize. You can use the fertilizer on potted plants, and I even used this homemade fertilizer on the plants I was starting indoors from seed.

### Tip #9—Plant Perennials

A perennial is a plant that returns year after year. After the initial investment, a perennial can give years of harvest. Asparagus, grapes, and berries are the most popular edible perennials. Many perennial vegetable plants have outlived the gardener who planted them.

Do some research before planting perennials. Some, like blueberries, need special soil conditions. Choose varieties that grow well in your climate. These plants are going to be around for years to come, so don't skimp on soil preparation. The biggest challenge for perennials is keeping them weed-free, so go ahead and mulch well when you plant them.

Our red and yellow raspberry patch was one of the best investments we made. We began with only a couple plants. Every year, we dug up a few of the side shoots and extended our row. Besides pruning them down to the ground in the winter and keeping them mulched for weeds, the plants take very little care. Raspberries are expensive to buy at the store and our investment has been paid many times over.

### Tip #10—Save Water

If you have to purchase water, or if your water use is restricted, saving water will be important to you.

Building up your soil will help reduce your need to water. Compost will help your soil retain moisture like a sponge. Good soil will also grow stronger plants which will be better able to withstand drought. Mulch will also help you hold in ground moisture.

Raised beds and container gardens look nice but take far more water. Plant directly into the ground to reduce your need to irrigate.

Avoid overcrowding plants. Remember that your plants are growing roots underground as big as the plant above ground. If you increase the spacing between plants, the roots will not have to compete for moisture. It can be tempting to crowd plants in hopes of receiving a higher yield, but your plants will be less healthy, prone to disease, and need far more water.

### Tip #11—Walk Your Garden

There is an old saying, "The best fertilizer is the feet of the gardener." It costs nothing but a little time to walk through your garden, but there are many benefits. You will be aware of what tasks need to be done. At the height of harvest season, missing even a few days in your garden may mean that some produce will overripen and go to waste. Zucchini has a way of growing to monster size overnight. Many times I have walked out to the garden for an onion and staggered in with more produce than my arms could carry.

If you want to avoid chemicals, preventive maintenance is the key. It isn't hard to pick off a few potato bugs, but when allowed to multiply, they can be hard to eradicate. With regular visits, you can be aware of the need to water, or see if the groundhogs are helping themselves to your buffet.

But maybe the most important reason to walk through your garden is enjoyment. Most of us garden because we want to. Of course, the food tastes better and the price is right, but, unlike our pioneer grandmothers, we would probably have something to eat this winter even if we had no garden.

So carry your morning coffee and Bible outdoors. Set an old chair or bench by the garden. Get eye level with your toddler and watch an earthworm wiggle into his hole or a honeybee buzz into a squash blossom. Take time to appreciate the world God created. And thank Him for the blessing of homegrown food.

# Shopping?
## We Live
## Off the Land

E MARTIN

A while ago a group of friends was discussing where they do their grocery shopping. "Shopping?" my sister said with a laugh. "We live off the land!" The phrase stuck, and whenever we decide to use what we have in the garden instead of grabbing a head of lettuce or broccoli at the store, we smile and say, "We live off the land."

Of course, we don't always "live off the land," and I couldn't blame my sister's friends for teasing her about it when they caught her buying powdered milk because the cow was dry.

What is it like to "live off the land"? Going to town with Mother was a special treat when I was a little girl. Her shopping cart was never very full, and since I'm older I've tried to compare it with the well-rounded carts I've seen others fill. What makes the difference?

I notice many shoppers pile their carts high with prepackaged foods. Although Mother bought sugar, yeast, baking powder, and a few other baking supplies, by far the most of our food was grown on our farm. I cannot imagine what a grocery bill would be like if all the food for a growing family needed to be bought at the store.

The family cow supplied us with milk, butter, cheese, yogurt, and homemade cornstarch pudding. Sometimes we even fed the cow the grass clippings after we mowed the lawn, reducing the cost of feed.

We had a flock of laying hens, so we never needed to buy eggs. Table scraps, sour milk, and trimmings from the vegetables were cheap chicken feed. For our flock of 150 laying hens table scraps were not enough though, and we also bought some chicken feed at the mill.

The flour for our homemade whole wheat bread was milled by a neighbor who grew the wheat himself. Every winter we butchered three fat hogs for our yearly supply of meat. During the summer we raised a variety of vegetables in our large garden. We filled pails with beets, carrots, and turnips, and stored them in the cellar for winter use. Heaps of cabbage, squash, and sweet potatoes were stashed away to eat after the garden was plowed for the winter, as well as fruit from our own orchard. Don't you agree, ours was a life of richness?

I've noticed another thing that fills grocery carts: cleaners. Mother saved a lot of money by boiling her own soap. Nowadays it seems we think we need a different type of soap for every surface we clean. I'm not sure why. That homemade soap worked well for doing laundry, washing the dishes, scrubbing the sinks, and mopping the floor. We even soaked a bar of homemade soap in hot water until it had a jelly-like texture, then used it to wash our hair.

If you would like to try making homemade soap, an easy way to begin is to buy tallow from a butcher. We are able to buy it for 10¢ a pound. Here is the recipe my mother used:

## Boiled Homemade Soap
35 lb. fat
6 lb. caustic soda
2–3 pails water
6 lb. salt

Put the fat, caustic, and about two pails cold water into the kettle stove. Heat to boiling. Stir frequently until all lumps are gone. This takes several hours. Keep a pail of cold water nearby to make the foam subside if it threatens to boil over.

When all the lumps have dissolved, stir in the salt. Bring to a boil, then add one more pail of water to cool it.

The following day, wear plastic gloves and use a sharp knife to cut the soap into bars. Remove the soap from the kettle and discard the poisonous brown liquid in the bottom of the kettle. Set the soap in a dry place to cure a month or two before using. It will not become sudsy in hard water but works well in rain water.

If you do not have a kettle stove, you might want to try one sixth of this recipe in a large kettle on the stove. Caustic reacts to aluminum, but stainless steel or iron kettles work. Be careful with the caustic—it's very poisonous. Unfortunately, it's expensive too. I've heard that pouring water over hardwood ashes, then straining it and saving the water produces lye, a substitute for caustic. I've never tried making soap with only homemade lye, but we did use some in addition to caustic when we ran out of caustic soda. I poured the dry ashes into a plastic feed sack, set it in a stainless steel pail, then poured boiling water over the ashes. A few hours later I lifted the bag out, leaving only the lye in the pail. Ideally, the lye is strong enough to eat the feather of a quill. If the solution is too weak it needs to be boiled down. Approximately one-third cup lye is needed to turn a pound of fat into soap. Sometime I'd like to experiment with making lye soap, but for now it's summer and the garden needs to be hoed. Maybe next winter…

# Just Looking

JANICE ETTER

Is there anything more sightly when the sun is shining brightly
Than a garden in the latter part of June?
It is ample compensation for those hours of perspiration
In the buzzing, heavy heat of afternoon.

Now the garden-keeper tarries near a spreading mat of berries
Where the bluish spikes of onions intervene,
Seeing shapely conformations with their many variegations
Of the not-so-plain-and-simple color green.

Here the melon vines are spreading and the broccoli is heading
And the squash will soon be filling out their bed.
Note the leafy convolution of a cabbage's solution
For the packing of itself into a head.

What a lovely place to linger! Pull a carrot's slender finger,
Hum the honeybee's enchanting little tune,
In the undisturbed seclusion and the glorious profusion
Of a garden in the latter part of June.

# Cooking
## on a
# Shoestring

DOREEN SEVESTREAN

So, you are cooking on a shoestring. Maybe cooking with a restricted budget has been forced on you through unforeseen circumstances. Maybe you've been cooking this way for so long you have run out of ideas. Maybe you have chosen to limit your budget as a way of simplifying your life and having more to share with others. Whatever your reason, whenever you are on a budget there are a few questions you face. What can I cook that my family will like? What can I do to keep from cooking the same old thing every day? How can I take this odd assortment of ingredients I have on hand and turn them into something edible?

I still remember the morning I read Proverbs 13 for my morning devotions. We had been discussing together as a couple how we could simplify our lives so we could have more to give. Our grocery budget was not large, but it was sufficient. I used coupons and looked for sales, all the standard methods of stretching it to the utmost. I wondered how we could cut the budget more. As I read, verse 23 almost jumped off the page to me. "Much food is in the tillage of the poor: but there is that is destroyed for want of judgment." Hmm. I wondered what that could mean. And so I started looking at my garden, at my kitchen, and at myself. And I have discovered this principle to be true. Let me share with you some of the ways I have discovered to save some money in the kitchen. They are just simple ways, but I hope they can be a blessing to you as you implement them.

***Number One:*** Stop wasting the food you already have. In thinking about Proverbs 13:23, I recognized the problem of wasting resources. So I started looking more carefully at what was going on in my kitchen. I had always been taught to scrape bowls thoroughly and not just wash that extra teaspoon of batter down the sink. I remember my grandmother telling me that she could get a whole extra cookie out of the cookie dough that most people throw away! My mom always kept a bag in the freezer for dry bread. She could produce bread crumbs or croutons at a moment's notice and the old bread was never wasted. Another thing we had done as a child was to put all the leftovers that could possibly go in a soup into a bowl in the freezer, and when it was full we had leftover soup, often dressed up with a tomato or broth base and seasoned with our family's favorite seasonings. It was actually quite delicious. (Although as a child I never liked when it had lima beans in it!) Leftovers that can't go into the soup pose a problem for our family sometimes. Leftovers reheated in the oven tend to dry out and become unappealing. Or maybe there are not enough for the family, and so the leftovers sit in the refrigerator till it's time to clean it out, and then they get spoiled or moldy and eventually pitched. Sound familiar? One day I cleaned out the refrigerator and I was ashamed. The half jar of tomato sauce was moldy, bits and pieces of various leftovers were looking slimy and smelling uncertain. In the vegetable crisper I found a few half-rotten zucchini and tomatoes; and since we don't have an animal to give the garbage to, it all had to be dumped out in the woods. Proverbs 13:23 kept rolling through my mind. What could I do to prevent this from happening? The answer was simple. I have learned that if I clean my refrigerator thoroughly every week, and halfway through the week take a few moments to look through it and see if there is anything that needs to be used, I almost never have to throw anything away. And if this makes you groan and sounds impossible on your time schedule, let me tell you the happiest part of the secret...when you do this every week, the refrigerator never takes long to clean! A few swishes with a damp rag and you are done!

You can take this Proverbs principle further. What about food on plates that the children didn't eat? Are your children messy eaters and some of it is landing on the floor? Teaching children to be thankful for what is given them and to be neat and careful with their food is something that will help them for life, and it helps your grocery budget too!

One of the biggest helps in cutting back on your grocery budget is having fresh fruits and vegetables in your own garden. Maybe you have a small yard or live in an apartment. Could you set out planters with tomato plants or strawberries? Is it possible to plant lettuce in your flower bed? Or maybe you have the same problem I did. In trying to plant too many different things, I didn't have enough time to help any of them grow properly! I had to take a look at which vegetables we actually eat the most, which have the most food value, and which ones I can save the most money growing myself. Then I needed to put more effort into growing these. Vegetable gardening is common these days. But fruit is what becomes really expensive. Have you considered planting strawberries, raspberries, or other fruits? Many times you can find other gardeners or friends happy to give away starts. Do you eat a lot of applesauce? Consider planting some apple trees. If you don't have time to tend flower gardens and vegetable gardens take a look at your priorities and your budget and decide which one is more important for the needs of your family.

**Number Two:** Use ingredients you have on hand. You might be surprised how much food can hide on your can shelves, pantry, and freezers. Challenge yourself to a week (or a month!) of cooking only with ingredients you have on hand. You may need to buy milk, eggs, or other fresh items, but as much as possible try to be creative with what you have on hand. Take an inventory of what's on your shelves and think of the possible combinations. It takes some time to figure out menus with the possibilities on hand, but sometimes we have more time than money. Get out the cookbooks and look for recipes that use basic ingredients and substitute as needed to use what you have on hand. Some of our favorite meals have been created using this method! Be willing to try new combinations!

**Number Three:** Simplify your menus. Traditionally, we as plain people have a heritage of abundant, rich food. There is no need for dessert at every meal. If your family needs something sweet, fruit (canned, frozen, or fresh) is enough. Look for recipes that use basic ingredients. Cream soups and cheeses can make a casserole yummy, but they are also expensive. It is a bit harder to stretch meat if your family is a traditional meat and potatoes family. One thing we have done when meat is scarce and potatoes and vegetables are plentiful and we want to make the meat stretch for two meals is to place a serving of meat on each plate in the kitchen and then pass just the potatoes and vegetables. If anyone is still hungry they can have more of what is on the table and the extra meat is "safe" for the next day! Soups are wonderful budget stretchers if you choose recipes with ingredients you have on hand. Serve with bread and a salad and you have a delicious, nutritious, and cheap meal. Often protein foods are the most expensive, especially if you do not live on a farm and have your own meat. Beans and rice form a complete protein and are relatively inexpensive. Each family has different ingredients that are cheaper for them. What works for us might not work for you. Look at what you have available and start from there. I have found several very old cookbooks that are helpful because they use only very simple old-fashioned ingredients that are cheaper! Or ask your grandma or other elderly ladies what secrets they learned for saving money. They have a wealth of resourceful ideas if we only ask!

**Number Four:** Look for substitutions to replace expensive ingredients. Make your own biscuit mix. Whip up a flavored white sauce to replace a can of cream of mushroom soup. Make a homemade pudding instead of using instant. Make your own mayonnaise and salad dressings. Some of these things may take a little more time at first, but once they become a way of life they are no longer difficult. I have spent a lot of time out of the country, and many ingredients we are used to are not available in other countries. I discovered this was a good thing to help me become more creative in the kitchen.

**Number Five:** Make your own convenience foods. If you tend to pop open cans and boxes or other more expensive precooked items because you run out of time and need a quick dinner fix, try making your own. Spend a day a month making soup and canning it or putting casseroles in the freezer. Or if it looks too big to spend a day at it, when you are making a casserole, make it double and freeze the extra one. Then all you need to do is thaw it out and pop it in the oven on a busy day. Breakfast casseroles usually freeze well too. Some of our favorite soups to can are vegetable soup, bean and bacon, taco soup, chili, and beef and potato soup. Another favorite time-saving method is mixing up a big batch of pie dough and freezing it in portion-size balls. It is literally as easy as pie to thaw out the amount of balls needed and roll them out and make pies. Or if you have lots of room and extra pie pans, put your crust in the pan and freeze it already formed. Another time-saver is making your own frozen pizza. Prebake your crust just until very lightly browned (10 minutes or so). Add the toppings, slide off the pizza pan, and place in a bag and freeze. When you are in a hurry, pop the frozen pizza into a pizza pan and heat in oven until cheese is melted and crust is browned. Think about the foods your family likes best and see if you can come up with your own inexpensive homemade conveniences.

*Number Six:* Use your oven efficiently. The oven is one other kitchen expense that we often don't think of. Instead of baking a little now and a little later, try to bake several things at once or one after the other so you don't have to heat up the oven more than once. If you have a casserole in the oven for tonight, put some baking potatoes around it for tomorrow. While living outside the country, I struggled with a gas oven that was not very cooperative. It was tiny and tended to burn everything on the outside and not get things done in the middle. I learned that it is possible to convert many casseroles to stove top main dishes. If all the ingredients are precooked, just dump them into a large skillet and simmer, stirring frequently. Get creative! Try your favorite oven dish on the stove top or in a crockpot and see if it will work.

*Number Seven:* Cultivate thankfulness. If we take a look at the world around us, we realize how blessed we are. We not only have food, we have plenty of variety too. If you or your family are finding a simpler menu and less variety something to grumble over, think of others and be more thankful than ever for what you have. If we have to eat oatmeal for a week, how terrible is it really? Many places in the world, breakfast is always the same year-round, year after year. Are we perhaps spoiled by our plenty? Let's be a thankful, generous people!

## Butterscotch Oatmeal

This is our favorite way of eating oatmeal. I never liked cooked oatmeal till I discovered this recipe. It is so easy that our seven-year-old daughter can make it herself! Makes 2–4 servings. Increase it to fit your family's needs.

1 egg, beaten well

2 c. milk

¼ c. brown sugar

¼ tsp. salt

1 c. oatmeal

2 Tbsp. butter

On stove top stir together egg, milk, brown sugar, and salt; add oatmeal. Cook over medium heat until thickened, stirring frequently. Add butter and serve warm.

## Honey Oats Cereal

Some granola recipes can become expensive as you add dried fruits, nuts, etc. This one can easily be adjusted to use ingredients you have on hand. If you don't have nuts, or seeds, or fruit, add the equivalent amount of oatmeal or whatever other ingredients you wish to add.

3 c. uncooked oatmeal

1 c. wheat germ

2½ c. chopped nuts

1½ c. sunflower seeds, sesame seeds, or pumpkin seeds

1 c. coconut

1½ c. raisins

1 c. honey

⅔ c. water

1 tsp. vanilla

⅔ c. vegetable oil

dash of salt

Stir together dry ingredients. Combine honey, water, oil, and vanilla; stir into dry ingredients. Spread mixture on baking sheet and bake 15 minutes at 350°. Stir and continue baking for about 10-15 minutes at 350°. Stir and bake about 10 minutes longer until nicely browned. Cool. Store in airtight containers in a cool place.

## Chunky Beef Soup

This soup to can is delicious and versatile!

2½ gal. water

2 lg. cans beef broth

½ c. sugar

½ c. brown sugar

¼ c. butter

1¼ c. beef soup base

4 qt. tomato soup

¼ c. salt

2 qt. flour

4 qt. finely chopped carrots

1 qt. finely chopped celery

4 qt. hamburger or beef chunks

4 qt. diced potatoes

4 lg. onions, chopped

3 tsp. pepper

Mix first 8 ingredients. Take approximately 2 quarts flour and add water to make a smooth paste to thicken mixture; heat to boiling point, then mix in vegetables. Brown hamburger or beef chunks and onions together (or have it precooked ahead of time). Add to soup mixture. Pressure cook at 10 lb. for 90 minutes or cold pack 2 hours. Makes 21 quarts.

### Bean and Bacon Soup to Can

4 lb. dried northern beans

2 lb. bacon

4-6 c. chopped onions

4-6 c. chopped celery

4 c. chopped carrots

5 Tbsp. salt or to taste

2 tsp. pepper

8 c. cubed potatoes

5 qt. tomato juice

2 bay leaves

Soak beans overnight; cook till nearly soft. Finely cut bacon and fry. Remove bacon and cook cut up onions in grease. Mix all ingredients together and heat until just simmering. Remove bay leaves before putting in jars. Pressure cook at 10 lb. pressure for 90 minutes or cold pack 2 hours. Makes 15 quarts.

## Corn Pie

This is a favorite summer recipe to use all that garden produce. To save more money, use your own recipe for cornbread.

3 c. corn

2 Tbsp. butter

½ c. chopped onions

1 lb. ground beef

3 Tbsp. flour

2 c. diced, peeled tomatoes

2 tsp. sugar or honey

2 tsp. salt

2 tsp. chili powder

½ tsp. pepper

1 box corn muffin mix

Combine all ingredients except for corn muffin mix and cook for 5 minutes. Pour into a 9x13 baking dish. Mix corn muffin mix according to package instructions. Spread over top. Bake at 350° until golden brown and toothpick inserted in middle of muffin batter comes out clean.

## Chicken and Rice Bake

2-3 lb. chicken legs and thighs

⅓ c. flour

2 Tbsp. cooking oil

1½ c. rice

1 tsp. poultry seasoning

1 tsp. salt

½ tsp. pepper

1 c. milk

2⅓ c. water

Dredge chicken pieces in flour. Brown in oil. Combine rice, seasonings, milk, and water. Pour into a greased 9x13 pan. Top with chicken. Cover tightly with foil and bake at 350° for one hour or until chicken and rice are tender.

Options: May add one can of cream of chicken soup for extra flavor and creamier rice. Or mix one recipe of flavored white sauce to substitute for cream soup.

### Mock Ham Loaf

1 lb. hamburger
½ lb. hot dogs, ground (or bologna)
1 tsp. salt
1 c. cracker crumbs
1 egg, beaten
pepper to taste
  *Glaze:*
¾ c. brown sugar
½ c. water
½ tsp. dry mustard
1 Tbsp. vinegar

Make glaze first. Then mix first 6 ingredients and ½ of glaze. Form into a loaf and place in a baking pan. Baste with remaining glaze. Cover to bake most of time. Baste a couple of times during baking; uncover long enough to brown nicely.  Bake at 350° for 1½ hours.

## Easy Fried Rice

Do you need a good way to use leftovers? You can stir leftover meat (of any kind) into this recipe instead of the chicken breast the recipe calls for. Also leftover drained vegetables (such as peas, corn, green beans) can be used quite easily as well. Don't have green onions? Just chop a regular onion and add to mixture. You can also add leftover scrambled eggs. The possibilities are nearly endless. Pass the soy sauce for more flavor!

1 lb. boneless chicken breast, cut in small pieces

4 Tbsp. soy sauce

1 Tbsp. brown sugar

1 Tbsp. cornstarch

2 Tbsp. vegetable oil

3 whole green onions, chopped

3 c. grated carrots

6 c. cooked rice

Marinate meat in soy sauce, brown sugar, and cornstarch for 30 minutes. In a skillet heat oil, then add chicken and onions. Cook about 5 minutes or until chicken is no longer pink in middle, stirring constantly. When tender add carrots and cook 2 minutes, stirring. Add rice and cook until well mixed.

## Hamburger Cabbage Rice Casserole

Wondering what to do with that bountiful crop of cabbage? Try this easy recipe.

1 lb. hamburger

1 onion

1 red pepper (optional)

½ tsp. salt

¼ tsp. black pepper

4 c. cabbage, cut up fine

¾ c. rice, uncooked

1 qt. tomato juice

2 tsp. chili powder

Brown hamburger, onion, and pepper. Season. Cook cabbage and rice on stove with tomato juice until rice is soft but not sticky. Mix cooked cabbage and rice with hamburger and put in a greased baking dish. Bake at 350° for 1 hour. Serve with sour cream if desired. Serves 8-10.

## Zippy Beef Zucchini Bake

This recipe is versatile. Easy to do in the oven or on stove top. Use beef or leftover chicken, whichever you want.

¾ lb. ground beef
1 medium zucchini, thinly sliced
1 can mushrooms (very optional)
1 small onion, chopped
1 Tbsp. butter
1½ c. cooked rice
1 can green chilies (or ½ c. chopped green bell pepper)
½ c. sour cream
1 c. cheese, divided
1½ tsp. chili powder
1 tsp. salt
¼-½ tsp. garlic powder

In a large skillet cook beef until no longer pink. In another skillet sauté zucchini, mushrooms, and onions in butter until tender. Add to the beef. Stir in rice, chilies, sour cream, ½ c. cheese, and seasoning. Bake in a 2-quart baking dish at 350° for 15 minutes. Sprinkle with remaining cheese and bake for 5 more minutes. Yield: 4 servings.

Options: Use 2 cups chopped cooked chicken instead of beef.

Option 2: Use as a skillet dish and simmer in a large skillet, stirring frequently, until heated through. Sprinkle cheese on top at serving time.

## Taco Salad Dressing

This is our favorite salad dressing. We use it for any lettuce or spinach salad, not just taco salad!

¾ c. sugar

1 c. salad oil

⅓ c. vinegar

⅓ c. ketchup

1 tsp. salt

1 tsp. celery seed

1 tsp. paprika

1 Tbsp. grated onion

Mix all together.

## Commercial Pie Dough

This makes a batch large enough to freeze some for next time!

5 lb. flour

4 tsp. salt

4 tsp. sugar

4 tsp. baking powder

3 lb. butter flavor Crisco

2 eggs

2¾ c. cold water

2 Tbsp. vinegar

Mix dry ingredients; cut in Crisco. Beat eggs; add vinegar and water to eggs. Stir into dry ingredients gently. This is a soft dough. I roll it between wax paper. Can be kept up to 2 weeks in refrigerator or frozen in pie-size portions and thawed in refrigerator later. Makes at least 10 double-crusted pies.

## Honey Mustard Dressing

Another favorite homemade dressing. Delicious on bean salad!

1 c. salad dressing (or mayonnaise)

¼ c. mustard

¼ c. vegetable oil

¼ c. honey

⅛ tsp. onion salt

¾ tsp. vinegar

½ tsp. garlic salt

pinch of red pepper

Blend together.

## Biscuit and Baking Mix

10 c. flour

½ c. baking powder

1 tsp. cream of tartar

1¼ c. powdered milk (optional)

3 tsp. salt

¼ c. sugar

2¼ c. shortening

Mix dry ingredients together. Cut in shortening until you have fine crumbs. Store in a tightly covered container. Use just like you would use Bisquick.

## Basic White Sauce

4 Tbsp. butter

3–4 Tbsp. flour

2 c. milk

½ tsp. salt

¼ tsp. pepper or paprika

Melt butter over low heat. Blend in flour, then slowly whisk in milk. Season with salt and pepper; cook and stir the sauce until it is smooth and boiling. Makes 2 cups.

May add any of the following for extra flavor:

chicken or beef bouillon

*continued on next page...*

celery salt

seasoned salt

1 tsp. lemon juice

½ tsp. Worcestershire sauce

1 tsp. onion juice

2 Tbsp. chopped parsley

2 Tbsp. chopped chives

2 Tbsp. finely chopped chicken

2 Tbsp. finely chopped mushrooms

cheese

### Breakfast Sausage

This is my favorite homemade sausage. Can easily be adapted to fit your taste.

2½ tsp. dried sage

1½–2 tsp. salt

1 tsp. pepper

¼ tsp. marjoram

1 Tbsp. brown sugar

¼ tsp. cayenne pepper

1 pinch ground cloves

2 lb. ground pork

Mix seasonings and sprinkle a bit over meat, mixing in, and then sprinkle more seasoning. Keep it evenly mixed. Flavor is best if you let it set overnight. Try adding a bit more sage or maple syrup instead of brown sugar, or for a spicier kick add red pepper flakes instead of cayenne. Have fun and experiment and don't forget you can use this with ground beef or turkey if you don't eat pork!

# How Do You **Manage?**

MARY E MARTIN

Too often in our plain communities, the "good managers" judge the "poor managers" as being lazy, sloppy, and slow. The "poor managers" judge the "good managers" as being selfish, materialistic, and inconsiderate. The call here is to remember that though there may be differing gifts among us, we are not to compare ourselves among ourselves. After all, we are all "good managers" in one way or another. May we all manage our lives in such a way that on the great day we can hear these words: "Well done… enter thou into the joy of thy Lord."

Some good managers dust their house once a week, because they like to know that they cleaned their house thoroughly; but they don't have time to bake bread for their family. Some good managers don't dust their house until they can see it needs dusted, because they are too busy (baking bread?) to do a job that doesn't need done. One day a very particular aunt stops in and sees where young son wrote his name in the dust.

Some good managers send mail to Grandpa on his birthday—not the day after—because they know how important mail is to a lonely old man; but their family only gets soup for dinner that day. Some good managers make a special meal for their busy husband, because they know the way to a man's heart is through his stomach; but they didn't get any mail sent to Grandpa until a week later (or maybe not at all?).

Some good managers fold up their sewing machine every day,

because it looks untidy to let it sitting out; but then they have to take time to get it back out the next day. Some good managers let their sewing machine out all the time, because they don't want to waste time getting it in and out. But then they walk past a "messy" sewing machine all day.

Some good managers set a day to clean the garage and then do it even if it's drizzling rain, because it seems impossible to find a perfect day. But then they need to work in the drizzle. Some good managers don't clean the garage until circumstances are right and the sun is shining, because they don't want to have to stop halfway through; but then it doesn't get done until six months later.

Some good managers always have the toys picked up before going to bed, because they sleep better knowing the house is clean; but sometimes the children have to miss their bedtime story. Some good managers tidy up the house in the morning, because both mother and children are fresher in the morning. But Daddy stubs his toe when he gets up at 2:00 A.M. to get a drink for his two-year-old.

Some good managers make 300 plus doughnuts on doughnut day, because they want their family to enjoy doughnuts out of the freezer for awhile; but the mess isn't totally cleaned up by bedtime, and Mom is too tired. Some good managers make 100 doughnuts on doughnut day, because they want the mess cleaned up by 2:30 and enough time for a nap before milking time; but their family only enjoys six or eight meals of doughnuts.

Some good managers only make one or at the most two school dresses for their daughters, because dress material is expensive; but then they need to wash dresses every other day. Some good managers make at least three school dresses for their daughters, because they have five girls to wear them out, and they don't want to get caught some busy week without a clean dress; but they have more money wrapped up in dress material.

Some good managers use the quiet hour while children are resting to tidy up the house, because that's the only chance they have; but then by evening they can hardly wait to roll into bed. Some good managers use the quiet hour to rest while the children are resting, because that's the only chance they have to catch up on some sleep; but then Daddy comes home to a cluttered house and spends his evening helping with the little ones.

Some good managers are always ready to send a daughter (or go themselves) to help a neighbor in need, because they remember the time someone did it for them; but then they hear that "neighbor to the west" considers them a poor manager because of how neglected their garden is. Some good managers make sure they have their own garden weeded before they run off to help the neighbor weed his, because the Bible says, "He that careth not for his own is an infidel;" but the neighbors soon learn not to ask them until the options are running out.

Some good managers don't know they are good managers, because no matter how hard they try they are not as efficient as "neighbor to the west," but remember the "last shall be first in the kingdom of heaven." Some good managers do know they are good managers, because they are able to stick to a schedule and get finished what they wanted to in a day's time. But beware, lest in the care of themselves and their family, they neglect the sick and the imprisoned.

# Give, and it shall be given unto you;

good measure, pressed down, and shaken together,
and running over, shall men give into
your bosom. For with the same measure that ye mete
withal it shall be measured to you again (Luke 6:38).

# Immortal
## Riches

ANONYMOUS

I stood in front of my sister's open cupboard and looked enviously at the contents. Parmesan cheese, chocolate chips, pretzels, spaghetti, and other things that hadn't been in my house for a long, long time. How good it all looked!

Guiltily I checked to make sure she was still in the basement. After all, I had come to help her for the day, not to stand and stare at her groceries. I swallowed hard and went back to peeling potatoes for lunch.

There was just no way around the penny pinching we needed to do to stay ahead on the farm. My shopping this morning had been severely limited to the basics, and I had been fortunate to walk out of the store with $2.00 left.

"How's your financial state by now?" asked my sister, coming up behind me unawares.

I jumped, then laughed. "How did you know what I was just thinking about?"

"I've been meaning to ask all morning," she said. "I knew you were having a struggle in the spring, and now it's been a dry summer."

I kept my back turned so she wouldn't see the bleak expression on my face. "It's pretty hard," I admitted. I didn't tell her I had been eyeing her groceries. Compared to a lot of people she did well and was a good steward. But they were not driven by necessity like we were. "But really," I added quickly, "the only time it's hard to be poor is when I want something."

We laughed, but as I said it I realized how true it was. Never had there really been a time we didn't have enough to eat or to wear. Our needs were still being supplied by God; it was the wants that were being crowded out. How much did wants really matter?

Sometimes a lot. Like not being able to afford a new dress for a sister's wedding. Like when the phone rings and someone wants to take sub orders for a benefit bake sale when there's not a dollar in the house. Like when you go yard sale-ing with your neighbors, who decide to buy bags of clothing for the people in Romania and you are too poor to pay your $5.00 share in the deal.

Oh, yes, there are definitely times when wants seem very important.

I sighed and bit the end of my pen unthinkingly. My mind was engrossed in trying to stretch the milk check to its utmost. Paying bills was never my favorite job, and this month was worse than usual. A tractor overhaul had been unavoidable. The mechanic had been good enough to give us three months to pay it, but it was still a sizable chunk each month.

My mind went over all the equipment on the farm. Did we have anything we could sell to make money? How blissful a large check would be right now! But the only thing I could think that was unnecessary enough to sell was the old, extra wheelbarrow sitting in the shed. That probably wouldn't even pay the mechanic to pick up his wrench. I gave up the selling idea.

What about making some money? But even as that idea came to my mind I had to reject it. I had tried once. Sewing had seemed like a good way to get some extra income, but it seemed every time I sat at the sewing machine the children felt neglected. The hassle hadn't been worth it.

No, the only way would be to keep on penny pinching. Borrowing Sunday shoes for Junior would be hard on my pride, but it could be done. I had grown my own navy beans, so we would just have to eat more beans.

So many things had changed in the past two years since we bought the farm. Store-bought cereal had gradually disappeared from the table, replaced by oatmeal and granola. Bouillon cubes and mustard were added to the list of luxuries. Jar lids were boiled in soda water to eke out one more use. Cakes didn't have icing, and fruit was canned without sugar.

I found that the area that was most profitable for me to penny pinch in was the kitchen. Our appetites governed that part of our spending, so it was also the hardest place to scrimp and save. It helped to butcher and process our own meat and make our own butter, but the best way was still to just not buy those things that we had thought were necessary before we bought the farm. Once we were willing to deprive our taste buds a little we found we could easily do without instant pudding, cream cheese, snacks, hot dogs, cream soups, etc. No, it wasn't easy, but it could be done.

I slipped my foot into a plastic grocery bag before I pulled on my boot. There, that would at least keep my sock dry. There was a crack in the sole where moisture seeped up through once in a while, and the boot was afflicted with two other holes as well. I grimaced at the ratty look, and my mind was busy as I started for the barn. Surely new boots were a need. I needed to have dry feet, didn't I? But as pictures of the footwear on the people in the Christian Aid Ministries newsletter flashed through my mind, I decided differently. New boots at this moment were not a need. I could keep on wearing a plastic bag until we managed to scrimp up enough money for a new pair.

I looked up at the starry, early morning sky. "Teach me to be content, O Lord."

I opened the barn door and met bad news. A cow had died during the night. A thousand-dollar cow. My shoulders sagged and the familiar tightness gripped my insides. In my mind's eye I saw a whole stack of bills, and the too-small milk check beside it. Oh, no. How could we handle such a loss?

My husband didn't have much to say, but I knew he felt the tightness too. Still, we could be thankful it was only a cow, I supposed. And at least it wasn't our best milker. But why *now*, when we were barely above sinking level…

This business of being poor was not easy. The rest of the world went by with money fluttering from their fingertips, it seemed. Here we scratched, scraped, and struggled to make the farm payment each month.

Still, we were doing what we liked—farming. And when I really stopped to think of it, there were many blessings in being poor too.

It taught us to be thankful. It taught us self-denial, and surely in the midst of our struggles we were learning to trust that God would provide.

There were also temptations in being poor. While richer people spent as they pleased, we were tempted to envy. And it was hard to say "no" to the temptations, to be adding extra income here and there, and making ourselves too busy.

The struggles of penny pinching are very real and can hardly be discussed with someone who doesn't know how it is. Most of us would really not choose this route if we had a choice.

A verse in 2 Corinthians 6 means a lot… "As sorrowful, yet always rejoicing; as poor, yet making many rich; as having nothing, and yet possessing all things" (v. 10).

Oh, yes, no matter how much penny pinching and saving we must do, we are rich! We have our faith in God, and that is enough. No amount of poverty can take that from us.

We possess all things! The riches of salvation through Christ, the peace that passeth all understanding, and best of all, the hope of eternal life.

Poverty can never touch our immortal riches!

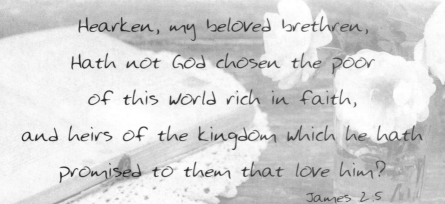

Hearken, my beloved brethren,
Hath not God chosen the poor
of this world rich in faith,
and heirs of the kingdom which he hath
promised to them that love him?

James 2:5

# Building a Marriage
## Without Draining
### Your Wallet

GINA MARTIN

When the schedule is full and the wallet is not, how do you keep love and romance in your marriage?

Is it a weekly date night? Romantic weekends away from home, just the two of you? Roses and cards on anniversaries? Should you find a special gift that will show your love?

All these things are enjoyable, but are they necessary for a good marriage? In some marriage articles I read, these items are on the priority list. I can begin to feel that if my husband and I can't do a weekly date night, our marriage is doomed.

But what if the family budget can't squeeze out money for expensive gifts or dining out? What if trustworthy babysitters are not available? Does it mean I have to be contented with a mediocre marriage?

Absolutely not. I know because I observed my parents' marriage.

My parents were busy dairy farmers with nine children. Since my grandparents were elderly and could not easily babysit, date nights without children were a rare occurrence for my mom and dad. As we grew, the older children could babysit the younger, and my parents had more opportunities to go away alone, but certainly not weekly.

And romantic weekends away without children? The first time I can recall my parents going away overnight by themselves was on their 25th wedding anniversary, and then for only one night.

Would it have been wrong for them to go away more often? Of course not. But was their marriage harmed because they didn't? I don't think so. A marriage is built on so much more than date nights.

I never doubted my parents were in love. On summer evenings, Dad would come into the house and say to Mom, "Let's walk out and check the corn." Hand in hand, Dad and Mom would amble over the hill, talking. (I presume about more than corn.) We children knew better than to tag along, though my parents were within earshot if help had been needed. This was their time together and is only one example of how they carved out time to build their relationship. And it cost nothing.

Time together to communicate is important for a marriage. For some couples, maybe a regular evening away from home is the best way they have found to connect. An inexpensive option that my husband and I have enjoyed is to swap babysitting with friends. We keep their children one evening and they keep our children another evening so we both enjoy some couple time. With the demands of young children, it is enjoyable to have an uninterrupted conversation occasionally.

Our date nights are not elaborate. Sometimes we take a picnic supper to a park and enjoy a quiet walk. Or maybe we poke around in a used bookstore on a winter evening and bring home a worn treasure for a few dollars. Often we take along our calendar and spend some time evaluating the last few months and making some goals. We have even returned to our own house, after dropping the children off, to enjoy a quiet meal together, though we do need to ignore the work we see.

Don't have easy access to childcare? Find other ways for time together. Try putting the children to bed early to create some couple time. We like hiding our favorite snacks deep in the pantry for our evening rendezvous. If your husband is an early bird, wake up with him and enjoy a hot drink and some conversation before the day begins. Maybe you can go along with him when he is running errands or take him lunch and eat with him at his job.

Spending meaningful time together should be a priority. Protect your schedule to make sure you are not overcommitted and are not too busy to find time for each other in everyday life. Though this may sound simple, saying "no" to good activities can be difficult and takes wisdom and willpower. Couples vary in how much activity they can handle without feeling stressed and disconnected from each other. Some couples love serving together in various ways and enjoy a busier schedule. Sometimes a wife married to a man with a different personality than hers will have to submit to his wishes. Strive to find a balance that works for you.

Even the best laid plans can go awry. My husband and I have had so many botched anniversaries, it has almost become a joke. It seems the more effort we take to make a special evening, the worse it gets. Soon after our marriage, a very special day for us found me in the midst of a miscarriage. We've had restaurant meals interrupted by the stomach bug. Hardly romantic! We have gone away for a night only to get an urgent call from my mom, who was babysitting, saying the children were sick and needed their own mother. Sometimes we almost fear to make extra special plans lest they be ruined.

Our most recent wedding anniversary was spent at a funeral. Later when I talked to an older lady at church, she said it is far more important what we do all year to build our marriage than what we do on our anniversary. How true. I'll take a good life together rather than an expensive date night with conflict the rest of the year. Maybe that is why the world emphasizes the externals, the gifts, and events, because they are missing the heart of love that comes when we suffer long, seek not our own, and are not easily provoked (1 Cor. 13:4-5).

It can be hard for us women to recognize our husband's expressions of love. Is he a hard worker? Does he make Bible reading a priority in your home? Does he show tenderness toward you when you are not feeling well? Does he help with the children or fix broken household items? Can we learn to appreciate these qualities as much as roses or a night at a secluded cottage? Maybe your husband likes to surprise you with special gifts. Or maybe he never remembers your birthday but also never holds a grudge. You have been given an even greater gift.

But when a friend talks about her weekend escape with her husband, or we see a bouquet of roses on her kitchen table, how quickly we can long for a husband that expresses his love in the same way. This is when we discover there are a few things that are required for marital happiness—and one of them is contentment. A discontented wife will not appreciate her husband's unique ways of showing love. When her eyes are focused on what she doesn't have, she won't see the blessings she already possesses.

A content wife will be a grateful wife. Gratefulness, combined with submission, forgiveness, and Christ-like love, is of immense value in a marriage. Study your husband and learn what pleases him. Never take him for granted. Show him appreciation and respect, and teach your children to do the same. While roses can show love, these character traits are far more important.

When your wallet feels thin, you can still build your marriage. A relationship is built by spending time, not money, and the greatest treasures in a marriage are bought, not with dollar bills, but with love and sacrifice.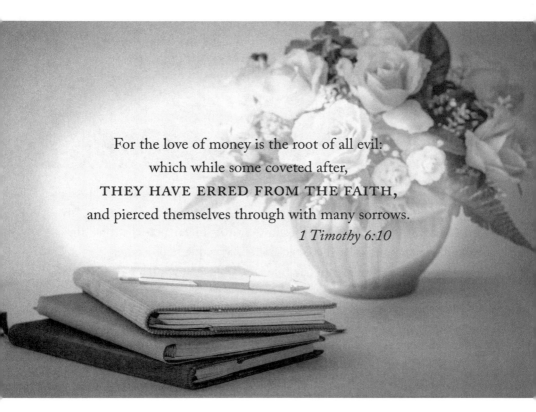

For the love of money is the root of all evil:
which while some coveted after,
**THEY HAVE ERRED FROM THE FAITH,**
and pierced themselves through with many sorrows.
*1 Timothy 6:10*

# THE Cheap Blues Cure

REGINA ROSENBERRY

I'm in a love relationship with my clothesline. No small outside clothes rack for me, for in the first month of our marriage, my husband built a clothesline. Sturdy metal poles; strong thin cable stretched tightly between them. I was one happy wife.

Give me a sunny, warm day. Give me a blustery March day. Give me a day with a foot of snow on the ground. I pull on my hubby's cast-off boots, gather up my wicker clothes basket, and crunch across the snow to the clothesline.

I breathe the icy air into my lungs as I hang pants with stiff fingers. They steam in the winter air and turn stiff. Fresh snow from the night before clings to the bare branches, making its own modern art with a splash of red from a cardinal in the center.

The wail of a train whistle floats across the frozen land, as I bury my nose in the fresh towels before I pin them to the line.

Ah-h-h, where else can I get a free drug for depression; a shot of feel-good serotonin? Where else can I go when I need a boost to fight the wintertime blues?

And then comes spring, and I follow the romance of the bluebirds. From wooing the missus to finding their home, it unfolds live in front of my clothesline. I peep into their box and admire the tiny blue eggs. A week later, after hanging up my sheets, I peep again and am awed by the ugliness of their firstborn.

I watch the apple trees burst forth their white glory blossoms in the orchard, and laugh at the comic show of newborn kids in the pasture.

Summer swings by, and now the laundry dries quickly in the penetrating heat. I stop to pick a handful of zinnias for the dining table, and watch a butterfly float by. After admiring the lace designs the tree casts over the grass, I drag my feet back into the house to eagerly wait for the next load.

Where else can I escape the endless march of dirty dishes, toy-strewn house, joyful noise of children, to find a slice of peace and quiet? Where else could I have a miniature get-a-way experience with soothing sounds of nature, and a warming bath of sunshine?

It's all free in my own backyard at the clothesline.

The benefits don't stop there. Mr. Sun saves money on our gas bill by drying my clothes for free. He kills bacteria, germs, and bugs on the kitchen cloths. Mr. Sun bleaches my whites, sucks out stains, and kisses my clothes with the freshest, natural scent to be found.

What joy when I crawl beneath my fresh sheets, to be greeted by this mixed scent of sun and bluebirds and flowers. It's the cheapest sleeping pill on the market.

Give me cold or heat. Give me snow or mud. Give me clouds or sun; you will find me hangin' out with my favorite friend. ●

# Faith in Twenty-Five Cents

## LOURA D NOLT

*"Take therefore no thought for the morrow: for the morrow shall take thought for the things of itself. Sufficient unto the day is the evil thereof."*
Matthew 6:34

Finances... Who of us can say we haven't been blessed? To live in the land of America is in itself a blessing. A country that has a civilized government, and though much of our country is immoral and has lost the value of godly standards, we are still very much able to live in peace, work in peace, and raise our families in peace. But again, finances... Surely those of you who have raised a family or are in the process of raising one understand that sometimes ends just barely seem to meet. That is the situation that this story takes place in.

The end of the year seems to do it to us every time. Things pile up and this year is no different. I can see the strain in my husband's face as we try to work out ways to scrimp some more, knowing that we do have many areas where we could definitely improve in being more frugal. With another sweet baby due, Lord willing, in a few months, we must get on a better budget.

In one week's time our furnace quit, three rather large bills came due, and then I had a fender bender with our van... Bills, bills, and more pending bills. Yes, it seemed too much. The checking account showed a big zero and I felt mounting frustration filling me as I watched my husband's frustration growing as well.

You see, I'm the type of person that struggles with thinking things need to happen quickly. Often I must remind myself to wait, slow down, and give God time to work. So quickly I can find myself wanting to fix it somehow, someway—and fix it now! Usually things go much better when I leave it up to God and keep my fingers out of it. But my mind worried on.

Our children must have heard us discussing the van and the estimated cost to fix it. Tonight, while I was working at the desk, doing some organizing, our little girl came quietly to me. She stood beside me and in a soft voice said, "Here, Mommy." She stretched out her hand and my eyes fell on a pile of pennies, a dime, and a nickel. "I want to give this to you, Mommy, to fix the van." Her voice shook as if afraid that I would think it wasn't enough.

It was twenty-five cents.

I wrapped my arms around her, eyes blurring, and thanked her from the bottom of my heart. That twenty-five cents turned into a million dollars. You see, it was still just a few pennies, a nickel, and a dime but my attitude changed. No longer can I find it in my heart to want to complain. How can I? We now have twenty-five cents more than we did before. And God worked in the heart of our child to provide that for us.

In her six-year-old mind that twenty-five cents would surely be sufficient to cover the cost of fixing the van. Her faith was strong, where minutes before mine had been sadly lacking. She had no doubt that God could use her money to fix what was broken. Do I have that amount of faith? Do I really believe the Word of our holy God when He says, "Therefore I say unto you, take no thought for your life, what ye shall eat; neither for the body, what ye shall put on"?

There was a big lesson for me in those twenty-five cents. Would I allow myself to worry and grow frustrated and irritable, or would I allow a simplistic childlike faith to guide me? Faith in the One who has granted us all these many blessings and has the right at any time to take them all away. *He* will supply our every need. *He* will be sufficient for our family. *He* is faithful and will be faithful whether I am in need or in plenty. Do I *really* believe that?

That twenty-five cents surely helped me put things into perspective.

May this twenty-five cents spread to you and everyone who needs to be reminded of Christ and His words, "Take therefore no thought for the morrow: for the morrow shall take thought for the things of itself. Sufficient unto the day is the evil thereof." Where our God guides, He provides. May you rest in that assurance as you strive to serve Him right where He has placed you.

# The
# Botched Budget

## FLORENCE FOX

Marlin frowned as he read over the credit card statement. "Honey, do you have any idea how high our credit card bill was last month?"

I tried not to look too concerned as I opened a can of crescent roll dough. "Was it higher than normal?"

"High enough. I guess your dentist bill was on there, too, but—whew." Marlin pulled the checkbook out of the desk drawer. "Providing for a family is not for the faint of heart or the unemployed."

I spread the dough into a cake pan and pulled cream cheese from the fridge. My family loved Peaches and Cream Bars for their sweet deliciousness, but I liked the convenient preparation.

Marlin's protests didn't worry me too much; he often made unhappy comments when paying the bills. I tried to be careful with my spending, buying only what we needed. I opened a can of peach pie filling and forgot about bills.

A month later, the credit card comments from the bill-paying corner were a little louder. "How did we spend so much?" Marlin asked me. "There are no doctor or dentist bills on this statement, and this bill is almost as high as the last one."

I had no answer. Surely Marlin could not be implying that I—trusted housewife—was the cause of financial damages. Marlin sealed the payment envelope and propped his feet on the bottom desk drawer. "You know, Honey, I wonder sometimes if we should start a budget."

I paged through my cookbook, sipping peach tea. "A budget? Isn't that what tightwads do? When I was young, a family at our school was on a budget, and everyone knew they wouldn't buy ice cream."

"Oh, I wouldn't cut out ice cream," Marlin said. "Maybe we would be more conscious how often we eat at restaurants, though. A budget outlines where the money will go. Otherwise, the money goes wherever it is needed by default. A budget would make it easy to see how we spend money."

Maybe I was guilty of more excess spending than I realized. But a family required so much food and so many clothes. If we did try a budget and ran out of money, perhaps I could prove to my husband how much it took to provide for a family. The credit card bills would be more understandable.

"Go ahead," I said. "Set up a budget. I'm willing to give it a try." I didn't think Marlin would do it; I thought a budget idea was just the result of a dismal evening paying bills.

Using a credit card was one way Marlin initially cut down on bill paying. In the first weeks of our marriage, Marlin instructed me to use the credit card instead of the debit card. "I'd rather pay one bill at the end of the month than subtract debits and save receipts all month long with a debit card," he'd said. We never allowed a balance to grow, but paid the total due every month. Had this attempt to make bill paying easier unintentionally become an unguarded system that made me careless?

Two days later, Marlin came home with an envelope full of cash. "Here it is," he said to me. "This is our spending for the month. I'll divide it into four envelopes for groceries, gas, giving, and medical."

I tried not to act alarmed. "That will last for the whole month?"

"Yes. How much should I put in the envelope for gas? We fill the van only once or twice a month." Marlin sat down at the desk and pulled out the money. "Oh, I can't wait to see a credit card bill of $50!"

I hoped Marlin was not going off the deep end. What if he didn't allot enough money for gas, and we would be grounded until the month ended and more cash was available?

Marlin cheerfully counted out a stack of greenbacks. "The amount for giving is already decided, because I could figure out the amount of tithe from my paychecks. How much should we earmark for groceries?"

In several minutes, Marlin had divided the money into four piles. "We didn't even use up all the cash I brought home," he said. "I'll put the remaining cash in an envelope marked 'extra' and that will be our emergency fund if we run tight somewhere."

The budget was established. I would do my best to comply with designated spending. After all, Marlin was not being stingy. The amount of cash he'd withdrawn for the month was almost as much as the last credit card bill.

We stocked up on groceries every three or four weeks, since our nearest supermarket was thirty minutes away. Between big shopping trips, we picked up what we needed at the local stores we drove past on the way to Marlin's workplace.

I had to run some errands the next morning, and since I was in town anyway, I swung by the store for a few groceries. We needed eggs, and I was out of butter. As I pushed the cart through the store, I remembered a few other things I needed. A bag of apples, lettuce, grapes that were on sale, pizza sauce, and sour cream also found a place in my cart. At the checkout, I fished in my purse for the envelope of grocery money and paid for the food. No swiping a credit card this time.

That week I left the house more often than usual, and two more times I made a quick trip into the local grocery store. Every time I picked up things we really needed, and every time I was surprised how high the bill was at the checkout. I began to feel a vague foreboding about how the grocery money would last. I did not want Marlin to know, but paying with cash was painful. After years of swiping a credit card and not paying much attention to the total announced by the clerk, hearing, "That will be $43.27," made my ears burn and my fingers ache.

Saturday afternoon, the children and I rode to town with Marlin on an errand to the hardware store. Since the hardware store was beside the grocery store, I ran in for a box of ice cream for the weekend. On the way home, Marlin asked me, "So how is the grocery money holding out?" I dug out the thin envelope of cash and started counting. The reality was shocking. I had spent half of our month's grocery budget in one week!

I was too embarrassed to let Marlin know my predicament. "It's a challenge," I said. "I think I'll spend less than before." And I meant it.

The next week I refused to leave the house. What if I was tempted to buy groceries? It was not hard to cook with what I had on hand the beginning of the week. By Thursday evening my options were running out. I found some shell pasta that had been in my cupboard a long time. The children do not like pasta, but I was willing to risk a few complaints at the table to save money. My new casserole didn't go over very well, and even Marlin commented, "Doesn't this pasta taste a little strange?" By Friday evening I was desperate. I thawed brats from the freezer, along with some frozen hot dog buns. The buns looked a little frosty, but they would have to do. Marlin has a sensitive tongue when it comes to freezer burn, and I was sure he would notice. He did.

"Are these buns old?" he asked suspiciously. "Mine tastes like it's got freezer burn."

"Sorry," I said. "My supplies are getting low. I'll try to stock up on my next trip."

"Do you still have enough grocery money?" Marlin asked.

Had the day of reckoning come so soon? And then I was cheered by one thought: At least he wouldn't fire me. "It's a bit distressing," I said cautiously.

"Oh, yeah?" Marlin looked curious.

"I spent half the grocery money last week. So the other half has to cover three weeks. That's why we must eat freezer-burned buns."

Marlin laughed outright. "Honey, we can adjust the budget!"

"But not after the first week," I said. "I'm still learning how to manage."

"You have lots of time to learn," Marlin said. "We won't allow a budget to make our lives stressful or make us eat old food. The budget is just a guide, not a chain."

I knew it before, but I discovered again that I have a very understanding husband. He was not angry at all.

Establishing a successful budget did not happen in one month. But I learned a lot from the practice.

Before using budgeted grocery money on nonessential items, I realized I must first buy staples like eggs, butter, rice, and flour. Next I would pick up produce, and last, what I called luxury items.

Marlin had been right; using designated funds did make it easy to track what we spent per month on gas or groceries. Before, I had no idea. Using cash made payment tangible; a credit card was too abstract and therefore inconsequential to me.

It was an accomplishment to learn that I could live within a budget. Once I saw the amount we saved, I was appalled by what I had spent before.

For me, there was one other benefit that equaled the satisfaction of saving money. It was to hear, on bill-paying night, my husband humming at his desk.

## Ordinary to Extraordinary
### LYDIA HESS

In the morning, fry some eggs,
Add fried bacon arms and legs;
Using ketchup, give the creatures mouths and eyes.
Carve a cuke into a boat,
Watch a pickle sailor float;
Gaze at clouds and point to pictures in the skies.

Save old cardboard tubes for crafts,
Cabin, fencing, hut, or raft.
Paper bags turn into villages and shops;
Bubbles blow through empty spools,
Crates make lovely desks for schools,
Bedsheets serve as mountains, planes, or carriage tops.

Whistle through a blade of grass,
Prove to some enchanted lass
That a row of water cups, when tapped, will sing.
Mothers' creativities
See the possibilities
And potential in an ordinary thing.

# Habits
# and Money

## GINA MARTIN

According to research, 40% of our actions are not made by decision but by habit. We don't consciously decide which shoe to tie first. Or whether to brush our teeth before or after our shower. Or if we should thrust our left arm or our right into our sweater sleeve first. But these actions, and hundreds more, are performed the same way each day because of habit.

What exactly is a habit? Charles Duhigg says it is "the choices that all of us deliberately make at some point, and then stop thinking about but continue doing, often every day." Habits are a blessing because they free our mind to think of other things. The first time we tied our shoe it took great concentration, but after years of practice we can put on our shoes while planning breakfast. Habits are the result of daily choices piled up day by day, week by week, year by year. These habits may be small, but their accumulation has a life-changing impact.

So what do habits have to do with money? Have you ever considered how many of your spending choices are based on habits? Often we spend money, or don't spend money, without consciously thinking about it. This can be a great blessing to our lives, or a challenge to overcome by the grace of God.

I was not aware of the formation of habits in my childhood home. My parents didn't talk much about wise money use, but they did model it. Their choices encouraged me to build habits that continue to bless me today.

What kinds of habits were given to me? Here are a few examples.

The Habit of Thrift—My parents taught us children to save until we earned enough for a desired purchase. If we wanted a new bike, we were not allowed to borrow the money. I saw my parents resist the pressure to buy an item just because it was "on sale" and prudently purchase only the things we needed. We learned to substitute and "make do" if we ran out of an item to avoid frequent trips to the store.

The Habit of Contentment—My parents were content to purchase used items when possible, accepted hand-me-downs gratefully, and passed on items to others. We were taught to appreciate simple homemade gifts where the love of the giver was more important than the value of the item. When my mother was tired at the end of a busy day, we didn't hear, "Let's order pizza," but saw her contentment in a simple meal such as tomato soup and toasted cheese sandwiches.

The Habit of Diligence—We were taught to work without complaining. Whether cleaning the house or pulling weeds, we were to do it "as to the Lord" (Colossians 3:23). We learned to care for our possessions, and mend and fix items when possible before purchasing new ones. My parents demonstrated skills such as simple home repairs, sewing, and gardening. My mother cut my brothers' hair and saved hundreds (maybe thousands) of dollars through the years. When I married, my mother taught the skill of hair-cutting to me.

The Habit of Generosity—My parents shared generously with others and helped me realize that many in this world have far less than I. Giving may not seem like a wise use of money until you read in the Scripture that it is "more blessed to give than to receive" (Acts 20:35) and "He that giveth unto the poor shall not lack" (Proverbs 28:27). Saving money so that you have more to spend on yourself does not bring joy. My parents showed me the value in saving money so you have more to share.

Good habits do have their limits. They cannot give you or your children eternal life. Salvation comes only by the power of Jesus Christ. But good habits do help everyday life proceed smoothly. Not only can they save money, but they also bring a sense of peace and security to a home.

When I married, I brought to my new home a gift of infinite worth, the gift of good habits. I expected to have a home where diligence, self-control, and contentment flourished. Thankfully, my husband brought the same gifts from his childhood home. These habits saved us money and helped us avoid some of the common marriage challenges that occur when a couple has grown up with conflicting financial habits (e.g., the saver married to the spender).

Maybe you weren't given the gift of good money habits from your parents. There is good news—the best thing about habits is that you can choose them. You can decide that you want to change your habit in a particular area and build a good habit in its place.

It does take effort. Today I helped my five-year-old learn to ride a bike. Learning to pedal, steer, brake, and balance is a real challenge. But I'm confident that with time (and maybe a few falls), the motions of bike riding will become habit, and she will ride almost effortlessly.

If you choose to begin a new habit, expect to fall a few times in the process of learning. Don't be discouraged; ask the Lord for help to try again. It may be good to begin with one area such as the proper use of credit. You could share with your children that there are areas in which you have failed, but by God's grace, you want to build new habits. Good habits passed down to the next generation have a worth that cannot be measured with dollar signs. ●

# 4 LEVELS OF Financial PLANNING

### MARVIN WENGERD

The way we grew up, our parents' concepts of financial planning, personal preference, and long-standing financial habits are powerful deciding factors to our approach to financial stewardship.

As an introduction to the Budgeting discussion that follows, here are four levels of Financial Planning most often followed. You will find yourself close to one of these. Looking at these four, then evaluating where you are at can help provide what direction your financial planning could take.

The first three are not financial planning in the truest sense, but illustrate the "plans" often used.

*The No-Plan Plan:* My income plus the money I can borrow from banks, individuals, and credit cards determine what I spend. I plan to do without a plan. Not paying bills on time is often part of this No-Plan Plan.

*The Paycheck Plan:* With the Paycheck Plan my income decides what I spend. If my income is $2,000 per month, I have that amount to spend on my obligations and whatever I perceive to be my needs. Nothing left at the end of the month? No problem, payday comes tomorrow. Do I have a raise coming? Great. The Paycheck Plan allows my expenses to rise with my income, assuring that nothing is left over at the end of the month.

*The History Plan:* I carefully record the money I spend so I know where every dollar went. The History Plan allows me to see what happened last month, and insofar as I am willing to be taught by history, I can make adjustments in my spending habits to bring them into line, even though I cannot "unspend" last month's spending. This plan increases financial awareness (in what direction does most of my money flow?) and often provides a necessary stepping stone to budgeting—hence its value.

*Budgeting:* Knowing what my approximate income will be for any given month, I sit down and allocate percentages of my income to specific categories (i.e. groceries, rent, mortgage, charity, savings, clothing, etc.) before I get my paycheck. I then purposefully live out the plan I have developed. While I am flexible to make adjustments to my plan if necessary (I am not money's servant), I am not willing to do so for every whim and fancy (I am not the servant of covetousness either). The purpose of my plan is not to exclude God from my finances but to curb the appetite I have for unsanctioned spending and to practice good stewardship of His gifts to me.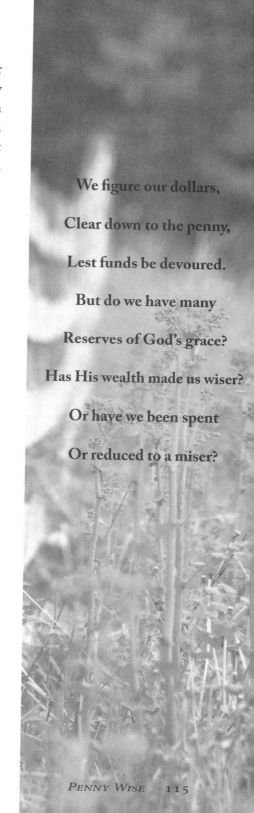

We figure our dollars,

Clear down to the penny,

Lest funds be devoured.

But do we have many

Reserves of God's grace?

Has His wealth made us wiser?

Or have we been spent

Or reduced to a miser?

# HOW TO
# Create a
# Family Budget

MARVIN WENGERD

B udget. The mere mention of the word makes some people's eyes glaze over. They imagine complicated mathematical formulas that one needs a math degree to understand. In reality budgeting is not very complicated—not nearly as complicated as the financial problems that come from ignoring this disciplined approach to finances. I promise you don't need to go back to school to learn how. I'll do my best to explain it in simple terms.

### The Foundation for Budgeting

The foundation for budgeting rests firmly on the pillar of faithfulness in stewardship. In Luke 16:10, 11 Jesus says, "He that is faithful in that which is least is faithful also in much: and he that is unjust in the least is unjust also in much. If therefore ye have not been faithful in the unrighteous mammon, who will commit to your trust the true riches?"

Here Jesus attaches my ability to be faithful with a dollar bill onto my capacity to be trusted with more important things.

Giving, paying my bills on time, caring for those in my house, not wasting money foolishly, not cheating on taxes, and being honest in my financial dealings all indicate a solid character that can be trusted with the weight of things that really matter—the Gospel, the care of souls, leadership, etc.

How do I get started?

Start with adding up how much money your family makes monthly. Add up paychecks, milk checks, and other income in an average month. Got that figure? Now let's say that amount is $2,400. Let's say at this very moment you hold that $2,400 in your hand in $20 bills.

Your next job is to decide how you want to spend that $2,400. What part of this $2,400 do I want to give to charity? Let's say that amount is $240. Put a paper clip onto twelve $20 bills and set them aside. Now let's say you have a mortgage of $700 per month. Put that aside on another pile. Out of the remainder you want to spend $260 on groceries—put that amount aside. Now you have $1,200 left for anything from clothes to travel to savings to medical. Get the picture? For a simple budget put each of these amounts into an envelope marked with its purpose. Throughout the month buy your groceries using money out of the envelope marked "groceries." You may not want to pay your mortgage in cash, so deposit that amount into a checking account and pay with a check.

There are many individual variables in budgets, and putting cash in envelopes may be seen as a tad outdated. But for many people it is a good way to get a firm grip on where their money goes. Additionally, it helps us make intelligent, informed decisions about how our money is spent.

To calculate and track your budget you can make your own lines on plain paper. Buy inexpensive ruled graph paper, or one of several good books to help you. Sometimes spending several dollars on a good resource provides the push we need to take our plan seriously. (After all, we don't want to waste the money we spent on the book, so let's follow through and do it!)

Now I'll show you two simple steps on the next three pages. The first is called *Create Your Budget*. The second is called *Track Your Progress*.

# Step One
# Create Your Budget

Total projected monthly income* for our family - $2,400

Using a graph paper, ruled tablet, or a form created specifically for developing a budget, spread out your income into categories. The total at the bottom cannot exceed your projected monthly income!

| Category | Amount Allocated | % of income |
|---|---|---|
| Giving | $240 | 10% |
| Mortgage Payment | $720 | 30% |
| Property Taxes | $168 | 7% |
| Repairs/Maintenance | $72 | 3% |
| Rent | ------ | ---- |
| Savings | $96 | 4% |
| Groceries & Household | $360 | 15% |
| Clothing | $240 | 10% |
| Utilities | $168 | 7% |
| Medical & Dental | $192 | 8% |
| Other Categories Unique to You | $144 | 6% |
| Total | $2400 | 100% |

Note: The above amounts and percentages are for illustration purposes only and are guaranteed to vary from one family to the next. Also, it assumes a horse and buggy lifestyle, and does not include car payments, insurance, fuel, and maintenance. Typically you need to lower your mortgage payment to 20% of your income (vs 30%) to accommodate a car in your budget.

*Note on "projected monthly income" – the projected monthly income must be what is called "take home pay." That means the amount you get after payroll taxes are taken out. If you're self-employed you could add an expense category where you calculated your total annual income tax and divide it by 12.

# Step Two

# Track Your Progress

Now, track every penny you spend. The dollar amount under each category is the amount we decided to spend in our imaginary budget on page 119. Keep this record on graph or ruled paper or purchase a ledger system from the resources on page 138.

For the Month of September 2014

| Date | Paid to | Paid with | Charity | Mortgage |
|------|---------|-----------|---------|----------|
| | | ck#___ □cc □cash | $240 | $720 |
| 9.1.14 | Any Town Bank | ck#124 □cc □cash | | $720.00 |
| 9.5.14 | Corner Grocery | ck#___ □cc ☑cash | | |
| 9.10.14 | Dr. How | ck#125 □cc □cash | | |
| 9.12.14 | Freedom Phone | ck#___ □cc ☑cash | | |
| 9.13.14 | Goodwill | ck#126 □cc □cash | | |
| 9.18.14 | McDonald's | ck#___ □cc ☑cash | | |
| | | ck#___ □cc □cash | | |
| | | ck#___ □cc □cash | | |
| | | ck#___ □cc □cash | | |
| | | ck#___ □cc □cash | | |
| | | ck#___ □cc □cash | | |
| | | ck#___ □cc □cash | | |
| | | ck#___ □cc □cash | | |
| | | ck#___ □cc □cash | | |
| | | ck#___ □cc □cash | | |
| | | ck#___ □cc □cash | | |
| | | ck#___ □cc □cash | | |
| | | ck#___ □cc □cash | | |
| | | ck#___ □cc □cash | | |
| TOTAL | | | | |

| Repairs | Savings | Groceries | Clothing | Utilities | Medical | Other |
|---------|---------|-----------|----------|-----------|---------|-------|
| $72 | $96 | $360 | $240 | $168 | $192 | $144 |
| | | | | | | |
| | | $40.00 | | | | |
| | | | | | $45.00 | |
| | | | | $36.94 | | |
| | | | $23.21 | | | |
| | | $14.40 | | | | |
| | | | | | | |
| | | | | | | |
| | | | | | | |
| | | | | | | |
| | | | | | | |
| | | | | | | |
| | | | | | | |
| | | | | | | |
| | | | | | | |
| | | | | | | |
| | | | | | | |
| | | | | | | |
| | | | | | | |

# A Financial
## Word to *Wives*

MARVIN WENGERD

- Be grateful for your husband's provision, be it little or much (Hebrews 13:5).
- Arrange yourself cheerfully under his provision.
- Avoid criticism when your husband makes a wrong financial decision—he will.
- Offer advice to your husband AFTER asking God for wisdom.
- Maintain a clear relationship. If you struggle in other areas of your relationship with your husband you become particularly vulnerable to unsanctified spending to fill the void you feel. You attempt to offset the pain you feel inside with the pleasure of buying. This exaggerates both problems: the financial and relational. (Husbands—you need to take the initiative to resolve these problems so your wife is not under this pressure.)
- If your husband needs financial help, do all you can to help him foster a good attitude towards those who are helping. Avoid poisoning the well by questioning their motives or planting suspicion in his mind about them.

# 15 Tips to Avoiding Financial Pitfalls

### MARVIN WENGERD

*A prudent man foreseeth the evil, and hideth himself; but the simple pass on, and are punished* (Proverbs 27:12).

1. Develop a detailed financial plan and live it out in the framework of God's call for your life.
2. Avoid surety—debt without a sure way to pay; co-signing is the most common form (Proverbs 17:18).
3. Spend less than you earn.
4. Don't hold finances as "natural" and thereby not subject to "spiritual" laws. Read Luke 16:10, 11.
5. Credit Cards—if you have a balance older than 30 days or if you are paying interest on credit cards, cut them up and get help now.
6. Never hide financial details from your spouse.
7. Denial digs a hole. Always have enough courage to face the truth.
8. "On sale now!" Be careful of becoming the merchant's best friend by responding to his sales.
9. Get good financial advice—don't ask just those who you think will agree.
10. There are basically two reasons people buy things: to increase pleasure and to decrease pain. Understand why you buy; the merchant does.

11. Crucify covetousness. It's sin.

12. Shop with a full stomach.

13. Be aware of and control or break your habits. Most of what you buy and where you buy it are dictated by the force of habit.

14. Logic often justifies what the emotions decide. Be cautious of making financial decisions when:

    a) You're under the influence of someone who knows this secret. Salesmen are masters at this and auctioneers often play the emotion strings as well. If they draw you into their product or position emotionally they know that most times your money will follow. Ask for time. Sleep over it.

    b) You're emotionally upset.

    c) You're under the emotional strain of false guilt (guilt is an emotion that can be good or bad) placed upon you by someone trying to reach into your pockets.

15. Be careful of where you have your attention—your money flows in that direction.

### *Security depends*
not so much upon
HOW MUCH YOU HAVE, AS UPON
*how much you can do without.*

Joseph Wood Krutch

# Defining & Achieving

## FINANCIAL FREEDOM

### MARVIN WENGERD

**1. Freedom from Debt**

Becoming or staying debt-free begins mostly with how you think. To develop a mind-set that causes you to arrange your life with little or no debt you need to abhor debt. As long as you remain on friendly, helpful terms with debt you will arrange your life around that mind-set. If, however, you reject debt as the best way to get what you want, you'll find that God will probably honor your commitment and help you find solutions that leave large debt out of the picture.

Living debt-free becomes a commitment to a lifestyle that influences almost all our decisions. This provides an excellent foundation for God to teach us the patience and discipline so often needed to live within our means. It is in this dependence-on-God mode that we learn some of our most valuable spiritual lessons. Learning daily dependence encourages the childlike faith God desires.

To become debt-free, first you need commitment to do so. Quit making excuses for doing nothing. Then ask wisdom of God to help you make a plan. Ask advice of others who have done the same. Then discipline yourself (this is usually not God's job) to follow the plan through good times and bad. Commit not to take on new debt.

**2. Freedom from Covetousness**

Covetousness fuels the engine of a credit economy. It's what makes us race with the Joneses while the Joneses race with the Millers and the Millers race with the Yoders. And all the while the joy so becoming of Christians dies on the altar of the latest fad.

There is a biblical solution for covetousness: repentance. Covetousness is idolatry (Colossians 3:5). Idolatry is an affront to the deity of God. God can free you from its green-with-envy grip. Once you are free of covetousness, contentment moves in. While debt doesn't always denote covetousness, if you replace covetousness with contentment you will find the temptation for debt diminishing. Being content confirms your trust in God's provision (Hebrews 13:5).

### 3. Freedom to Establish Treasure in Heaven

One of the most compelling reasons to avoid the debt-up-to-my-neck lifestyle is that it severely limits your ability to use your time and money to establish a heavenly account (Matthew 6:19, 20). The push behind becoming debt-free should not be to accumulate more for ourselves, but to free us up for God's service.

Living a debt-free lifestyle increases your options to give and go as God directs. With debt to the level of bondage you give your strength to the world's system and ideas and shortchange God (Matthew 6:24). You're bought with a price; be not the servant of men (1 Corinthians 7:23). To achieve this you must commit to hold this world's goods loosely. Train yourself to see yourself as a steward, not the owner. God gives. I use wisely. Ask Him for direction on how He would have you use His resources. In that way He will help you establish an account where moth, rust, thieves, and a down economy can't get to.

# A Tightwad Writer's Dilemma

STEPHANIE LEINBACH

I sorted laundry, tossing clothes into dark and light piles behind me, like a dog digging for a bone. I wasn't looking for a bone, but I was looking for an idea. Maybe I could find one at the bottom of the hamper.

The deadline loomed for the *Penny Wise* Keeper'sBook™. I couldn't think of what to write, but I wanted to submit something. If I could get an article printed in *Penny Wise*, then I would receive a contributor's copy. This copy was essential to me, because—well, because I was too much of a tightwad to buy one.

I held up one of my husband's socks. Holey. Beyond repair. I laid it aside to cut open and use as a rag. Cotton socks made great rags. Maybe I could—but no… When I was at a housecleaning as a teenager, another girl had held up one of my mom's sock rags and sing-songed, "Somebody uses socks for rags?!" I had wanted to die— just curl up and die beside the dusty radiator. Sock rags were not done, apparently, and confessing to them was embarrassing, even now, fifteen years later.

Penny pinching was only a pastime for me. Some women I knew made a career of stretching pennies, for love of elasticizing copper or—unfortunately—out of dire necessity. But I was a dabbler, a hobbyist pincher who saved pennies in all the expected ways. I had nothing important or earthshaking to say on the subject.

Frowning, I loaded the washer and measured detergent. My husband, an appliance repair technician, had taught me that a front-loading washer only needed about two tablespoons of detergent. Laundry, particularly towels and washcloths, will stink if too much soap builds up in them. But I couldn't write a whole piece about using less detergent and thereby saving money as well as keeping your towels smelling fresh. I'd have to come up with something else.

I dumped white vinegar into the fabric softener compartment. But everyone knew about the wonders of white vinegar, didn't they? My idea needed to be something smashing. Original. Clever.

Well, I had my Ultimate Shopping Tip for Tightwads: Stay home and substitute. But how original was that? Not very. And in four words, I could cover the subject.

What was the editor of *Penny Wise* thinking? In the spirit of frugal living, he should offer the book for free. How would all the non-writing penny pinchers cough up the money to buy a copy? It took a lot of courage to sell a book on saving money.

Maybe I could borrow a copy from someone. I had writer friends more prompt and inspired than I—Gina, Crystal, Regina. I would ask to read one of their copies. They were true and honest penny pinchers who would understand my dilemma. Nobody can get more miles out of a book than a group of tightwads, but don't tell any publishers I said so.

Books. Oh, that's right. I had a stack of library books to return on my next trip to town. Wait. What about that idea? A library is a wonderful resource for a penny pincher. If a local library doesn't have a specific book, a librarian often can track it down through interlibrary loan. Then again, I had several large libraries nearby, staffed with librarians I considered my friends. Not everyone would be so blessed. Besides, it took a lot of time to winnow the chaff on the library shelves in search of the grain. And maybe dyed-in-the-wool penny pinchers read only tattered copies of *The Tightwad Gazette*.

The deadline was probably past by now, so why was I spending so much time thinking about what to write? I picked up the hamper and turned to leave the laundry when I stopped, hampered by a worrying question: Did I qualify? Was I really, truly a penny pincher? I tried to be careful with our money and possessions, but I could do more. Probably. Definitely.

What had Jesus said about the woman accused of being wasteful? I abandoned the hamper in the laundry and sat down with my Bible. Mark 14 tells the story. A woman breaks an alabaster box of precious ointment and pours it on Jesus' head, and when the observing crowd murmurs against her, He says, "She hath done what she could." Not only that, but He calls it "a good work." An honor to her, a comfort to me. I also would do what I could, offering Him the broken alabaster of my life, knowing it was a good work in my Lord's eyes.

And this, too, I could do—thread words together like beads on a string. I would write and submit and see if I would be able to save 499 pennies—the likely cost of *Penny Wise*—to use elsewhere. The Keeper'sBook™ was called *Penny Wise*, not *Dollar Stretchers*, so its core message spoke of making a difference in small ways. Even I, a novice in the world of penny pinching, could contribute a voice of encouragement: Do what you can. It is enough—no, more than enough. It is, in the words of Jesus, a good work.

# A Lesson
## FROM THE
# Apple Orchard

### HR DUREN

**M**ama cheerily honked the van horn as she left the driveway. She was heading for work. I stared after the van, and as it disappeared my thoughts went down a well-worn track. *I wish she didn't have to go to work. I wish we had so much money that Mama could sit in a rocking chair on the front porch all her days reading her Bible and sewing quilts to her heart's content.* I paused in my thoughts, wanting to stay away from more dangerous ground, yet my mind brushed over it. *If only Mama had a husband to carry the heavy part of life for her.* I was ashamed instantly. Mama herself had told me that God was better than a husband and that He took such good care of our family that we need never worry or complain. She was glad for work. She liked working hard. And she has taught us, her two girls, to be thankful for our jobs, which, combined with her income, makes a comfortable living for our little family.

Then God brought to mind a story that has been told to me by someone who really knew what it was like to work hard, and still not have enough money. I heard the elderly lady's voice in my memory telling me about a day from her past. It brought me back over unfamiliar years to a time long before I was born.

It was the 1930s. Everyone was poor. Everyone had to work hard, and eat less. Families joined together to survive. It was a time when those who really had religion had strength and those who wore religion "got all prayed out." Discouragement, despair, and depression ran high.

It was the Great Depression, monetarily and mentally. But even hard times do not stop young people from being full of life and love. Two young folks were married, even knowing that they were going to be poor and would need to scrape to just get by. They felt rich in each other's love and managed to get through the first year, but the second year gave them a delightful new problem to provide for.

"We are down to the last penny," the husband said, "and we have nothing left to sell."

The couple sat in the semi-darkness of the early morning. They were at the kitchen table, only a thin slice of fried bologna on each plate.

"There is an orchard I heard of that pays 10 cents a bushel for gathering wind-fallen apples and 15 cents for picking from the trees," the husband said quietly.

The wife smiled. "That sounds good."

"Maybe if I worked all day, I could get a nice little sum." The husband glanced at his hands.

"I could go along and help," the wife offered.

"But the baby…" the husband began.

"He'll be fine. Together we can get more." She looked lovingly at her husband. "And it will be nice to work together."

It was only an hour or so later when the young couple with their baby arrived at the apple orchard. It was a beautiful day. The chilly night air was quickly being warmed by the encouraging sun. The wife spread a blanket out on the ground and laid their baby on it. There was plenty for him to watch, plenty to keep him quiet.

"You'll be good for Mother, won't you?" she whispered into his little ear. "Let's both help Daddy, shall we?" And with a kiss she left him.

The baby was content to lie kicking and gurgling. His parents talked to him and smiled at him as they worked nearby. The wife picked apples from the ground and her husband started to pick apples from the trees, but stopped after only a few minutes. The wife looked up questioningly.

"I can actually earn more by going faster down here," he said, tapping the ground with his foot. He smiled at his wife as he bent to grab up apples.

Their hands flew. They were getting quite warm now. To give their backs a break they would sometimes go on their knees. The husband carried the full bushels to the edge of the orchard. The wife would move the blanket and baby along with them. When the baby started to fuss, the husband told her to rest a moment so she could feed the baby. An apple or two and a drink of water was their lunch. They talked, laughed, and sang.

As the sun started casting long shadows they grew quiet and simply worked. Occasionally the husband would give an encouraging word to his wife. The sound of the farmer coming with his wagon and horses meant it was time to quit. The husband slowly straightened his aching back and helped his wife to her feet. She bundled up her baby and watched her husband top off her last bushel. The farmer ducked under a low branch and stood with one work-worn hand on the limb. He squinted at them and smiled.

"You got quite a few."

"Yup." There was an understandable ring of satisfaction in the husband's voice. "One hundred fifty-three."

The farmer's eyebrows went up and he glanced at the wife.

"You count them," the husband said, smiling. He knew he was right. They headed towards the waiting wagon and horses, the farmer and husband carrying the last two bushels. The wife, holding the baby and blanket, walked along behind the two men.

At the wagon the men began to load the apples. When they were done, the farmer shook his head.

"You sure did a good day's work. There *are* one hundred fifty-three bushels."

The husband rested an arm across his wife's shoulders. "She worked hard and the baby was good."

"You picked a lot more than I did," the wife murmured, but her face was rosy with pleasure.

The farmer opened his billfold and carefully counted out fifteen dollars and thirty cents. He shook hands with the husband and nodded at the wife.

Tired, sun soaked, and smelling sweetly of apples they went home, the husband with his shoulders back and head high. He felt a man again. The wife smiling, having had such a good day. They felt rich. Rich, in that they could work hard.

---

Years later the wife went to get her apples. She didn't need to pick them from the ground or trees. She went to Kercher's Orchard and chose some from big wooden crates. There were several other people there, all well dressed and well fed. It was the fall of 2010.

"They don't have the nice apples anymore," she said to Mama and me. "They don't have the good, old-fashioned kind." It was easy to be friendly to strangers on a beautiful fall day, and that was when she told us her story.

She ended with these thoughts. "Now we have plenty of money and the children don't know a thing about working hard for just the necessities. They always want more and they are never happy. They waste their money. Maybe they wouldn't waste it if they had to work as hard as my man and I had to." She shook her head sadly. "The children nowadays don't know what real work is, nor what real want is!" I never did find out their names, but the lesson that this sweet older woman's story gave me has stayed with me.

We live in a culture that says you deserve the best. Not only do you deserve the best, but you deserve it right now. The less work involved the better. Working hard has gone out of style as we become more selfish and self-pampering. People nowadays *love* fun and *love* comfort. If something is hard, we don't want to do it!

But it is important to know how to work diligently, because the Christian life can be hard. We are to follow Jesus on a path that goes through times of suffering. That is how God refines us and makes us useful. We know this and yet… are we accepting the idea of the world that life should be fun and easy?

I had let the world's idea of happiness slip in. I smiled sheepishly and whispered a prayer. "God, thank you for our jobs. Thank you for contentment and true happiness in serving You. And thank you very much for a godly mama who does everything 'as unto the Lord!'" ●

# •CONFUSING•
# Conclusions

DANETTE SHIRK

How do you pinch pennies?

I have often wondered about pinching pennies. How do you do it? By growing and canning all your own food, wear cloth diapers on your babies, and never buying ice cream?

Once, long ago, on a trip I visited two different homes. The first housewife, Lynda, lived luxuriously. She bought instant potatoes and used pampers and went with her family to McDonald's every Saturday evening for supper. Lynda and her husband built a new house and "decked it out." They bought new shutters for their house, and then decided they didn't quite like the color, so they stacked them up neatly, and went and bought prettier ones. They had a prosperous business and could afford all this and more.

Helen, the other woman, made all her own butter, never bought chocolate chips, and used a goat to mow her lawn. Helen and her husband lived in an old farmhouse with chipped paint and cracked linoleum floors. They did not make a lot of money and they lived within their means.

Lynda and Helen both were dedicated Christians and were concerned about raising their children for God's kingdom. Both were industrious and taught their children the joy of working hard. Both had happy homes.

And both talked about . . . pinching pennies! It was funny. Lynda and Helen were at opposite ends of the financial ladder. Their living standards had little in common. Yet each was concerned about making the most out of every penny they earned.

Once I sat beside a lady in church who had a terrible odor. I got very little inspiration from the sermon because of it. I had a hard time visiting with her later because there was this fog of smell between us. Imagine my surprise when she informed me that she does not wash clothes or bath very often. "It all just costs so much money," she sighed. "So I figure if we don't bath much, we are saving on water, and if I don't wash the clothes as often I save on *water and soap both!*" She seemed quite pleased with her discovery. I did not share her pleasure.

One day, Kendra (a non-farmer's wife) told me that she has trouble finding enough work for her growing sons during the summer months. "I could take the boys to help on my father's farm," she said, "but it takes too much gas to run them that far. It would just waste too much money."

Now when I go past Kendra's house and see her boys goofing off *on the road* I wonder if she is thinking straight. If one of those boys got hit by a car they could rack up a hospital bill which would cost more than several runs to her parents every week.

Evelyn planted lots of raspberries and strawberries for her family. Excluding the initial cost of the plants, and her time to water and weed, she basically feeds her family free fruit. But you know what? The fruit stand down the road from her house is selling berries for an exorbitant price. "What should I do?" she wondered. "I could sell my berries to them, and buy apples and peaches and still have a lot of pennies left over!"

Anyone have an answer for that? Then to complicate matters further, when I checked the price of peaches and sugar, I discovered I could buy already-canned peaches at the bent-and-dent store for less than I could can peaches myself!

What happened to the time-honored conviction that canning and freezing our own food is cheaper? *Confused* is stating this mildly.

Pinching pennies is so relative. Lena buys mushroom soup by the case, then uses free material and makes her own underwear. Karen would never think of buying mushroom soup, but then she keeps cheese on hand all the time. Darlene thinks cheese is an extravagance, but she buys boxes of oranges in the winter. Lena and Karen don't buy oranges because "they are too expensive and we have our own home-canned fruit."

Who is pinching pennies? I am not sure if I have ever talked to a plain person who did not think she was pinching pennies in one area or another. And you know what? Each one seems to think she is saving in the best way! Karen thinks Lena is extravagant for buying mushroom soup. Lena can't figure out why Darlene buys oranges. And on it goes.

Once when I was discussing this confusing topic with my sister, she said, "The problem is not how *we pinch pennies,* it is whether we *even pinch pennies at all!*"

Oh! New thought. So it doesn't matter if we buy ice cream, as long as we don't buy cream cheese, too? Just so we save somewhere. Put like that it doesn't make sense. If you are going to buy ice cream, you may as well buy cream cheese, right? And yet there is a subtle principle involved. A person who does not allow herself to buy everything she would like to buy is using temperance. That counts, in God's sight.

And yet when you think about it, which of us is *really* pinching pennies? If we are really, really pinching pennies, we would eat rice every day, and there would be no decision about whether we would buy potato chips. We'd have an outhouse, rather than our convenient bathroom, eliminating the decision of whether we should wallpaper our bathroom walls or put up tile. We would wash our clothes by hand, so we would not have to decide if we were pinching pennies by buying the more expensive wash machine which saves water. Possibly if we were really, truly pinching pennies, we would even pull our own teeth, saving some dentist bills!

How about that for a confusing conclusion?!

But 1 Corinthians 14:33 says, "God is not the author of confusion." How can we see some order in the midst of confusion?

I believe the real issue here is this, "Are we being good stewards of what God has given us?"

We can grow in our knowledge of how to be good stewards by reading articles on pinching pennies. We can learn from each other.

Mary Ann taught me that I am actually saving money by buying whole wheat flour (which is often more expensive than white flour) because it is much healthier, so I will (hopefully) eliminate some doctor bills in the long run.

Luetta showed me that using worn-out material to make my daughter a dress was not saving money. The thin spots soon wore into holes and I only wasted time. Better to use durable fabric in the first place, even if it costs more than free rags.

My husband assures me that sometimes it is okay to buy paper plates or convenient foods like bananas, if I need some extra minutes to minister to the needs of our children, or to have some quality time left for him. He says that is being a good steward.

But then, he does not believe it is right to buy a Milky Way candy bar every time we go to the grocery store. That is not called "good." That is called "intemperance."

Let's watch for ways to pinch pennies. Let's be good stewards of our gifts from God. Let's ask God and each other and our husbands how to best do this. Let's help each other through the confusing conclusions we bring upon ourselves. God will bless our efforts!

# {Resources}

**Books You May Want to Read**

*Managing His Money,* Samuel D Coon
*The Life of Christian Stewardship,* Books 1, 2, and 3, Dallas Witmer
(These titles are Lamp & Light Correspondence Courses)
Lamp & Light Publishers
26 Road 5577 | Farmington, NM 87401-1436
505.632.3521

*Regaining Control of Your Personal Finances*
*Regaining Control of Your Farm Finances*
Ridgeway Publishing
3129 Fruit Ave | Medina, NY 14103
888.822.7894

*Money Issues for Christians Today,* David L Martin
Rod & Staff Publishers
PO Box 3 | Crockett, KY 41413
606.522.4348

*Kingdom-Focused Finances for the Family,* Gary Miller
TGS International
PO Box 355 | Berlin, OH 44610
330.893.4828